Catch and Release

A personal quest to catch the truth and release the illusion about unconditional love

Joy Popma Gray

Catch and Release – a personal quest to catch the truth and release the illusion about unconditional love

ISBN: 978-0-9978391-0-4

Publisher: Joy Time Publishing

Farmer's Branch, Texas, USA

Edited by Susan M. Sparks

Cover design by Mary Pat King

This book is my opinion formed from my interpretation of what I've read, listened to, and experienced. I am only experienced in life and love as I have lived it. I believe I received a calling to share my very personal story and the enlightenment I have implemented into my daily life with others. While my story is true, the names are fictional.

To my son and my ex-husband

PREFACE

We are made up of a higher-self and an ego. The ego enables us to survive. Our higher-self is present when we connect with nature, compassion, love, and purpose. For most of my life my ego was in the driver's seat with only glimpses of my higher-self. I wasn't aware of how ego-driven I lived my life, manipulating others for my personal benefit.

I met a wonderful man on Match.com. We were together on and off for four years. We struggled with our own insecurities and expectations of how we thought the relationship should be. We went through the hills and valleys like most married couples go through, getting to know each other through the fun and all the differences in our character and lifestyles. We were a great match physically and playfully, but often lacked the skills in non-defensive communication. After the fifth or sixth time we broke up only to get back together, I felt we were becoming closer. He on the other hand, was beginning to question the relationship and our compatibility.

Could it be our own perception of the relationship, and the lack of communicating the differences caused the multiple break ups?

Was each of our internal dialogues creating fear and insecurity from the uncertainty of how the other truly felt?

Were we at different places on our path and the timing was off?

Was the relationship meant to be brush strokes in the big picture of my life, and he was not my forever partner?

I have asked these questions and many others while writing this book in order to discover my higher-self. Perhaps you've wrestled with some of the same questions I did.

Have you ever felt that if the relationship is too hard that maybe it's not meant to be?

Do you ask yourself why you can't get that loving feeling for a person you are with, even though they are perfect for you?

Have you chipped away at your partner's confidence and love for you, by picking them apart, and asking them to change when the truth was they didn't meet your fairytale expectations or timeline?

Have you sabotaged a relationship because you couldn't accept yourself as a worthy partner to the one you were with?

Do you accuse your partner of red flags that are your own as well?

Do you place blame on your partner because it is easier than looking at yourself and acknowledging you're the reason for your conflicts and failures?

I began writing to make sense of my own ego-driven actions. I share this book with those of you who want to get off the crazy train of our egos where drama and distraction cloud us from living our life with true purpose and love.

We are all capable and destined to live a life filled with love, joy, and enlightenment. It begins with accepting everyone on the journey of life and respecting that while we are all on the same path, we may be at different places while we work toward a life with love.

What I have learned through internet dating, and the stories shared with me from other participants, some successes and some throw backs, is the heart of this book. I hope my insight within these pages, help you find not only a great CATCH, but a RELEASE of the things that no longer serve you.

CHAPTER 1
FIND THE POND AND BAIT THE HOOK

In this age of technology we are no longer limited to the pond in our own back yard. We may cast our lines via email across the street, city, state, and continent. Technology gives new meaning to the saying, "There are plenty of fish in the sea." Choosing the pond for a fisher of men or women is unique to each individual. Today there are many choices with Match.com, eHarmony, Christian Mingle, and Tinder, just to name a few. I had not even heard of internet dating until the summer of 2011…

I had just moved back to Dallas from a small Texas town. My husband, Craig, and I were separating after seventeen years of marriage. I first mentioned divorce four years earlier when my brother had passed away from lung cancer at the age of forty-five. After his funeral Craig and I discussed the state of our marriage. We both agreed we were more like roommates than a happily married couple and life was too short for simply existing in our marriage. It would take a while to sell our house and work through the separation, but I encouraged Craig to not allow a piece of paper to get in the way of true love if he were to meet someone in the meantime. I know it sounds crazy, a wife giving her husband permission to be with another woman. Craig had always been wonderful, caring, and supportive throughout our marriage, and I truly wanted him to be happy. I wanted to be free to explore and create my own life. I felt if he were happy then I wouldn't feel so guilty about our failed marriage.

I was forty-two when I moved into my little home on the golf course. Craig helped me purchase it with the profit from selling our ranch home. I was a stay-at-home mom, so I still needed his financial support until I could get on my feet. I needed a job that could turn into a career. I had a knack for real estate. I had found the homes we purchased that only needed a little cosmetic work. I did all the painting, flooring and landscaping while we lived there. A few years later we sold it and made a nice profit. I was going to do the same thing with this golf course home, and I knew the dirt alone was a smart investment. Real estate in Texas was appreciating steadily. I thought maybe I should get my real estate license. I would sign up for classes as soon as I got settled into my new home.

I was raised in the big city of Dallas. I had longed to leave the city and live in the country, surprisingly I was excited about coming back and starting over. Craig and I decided coming back to Dallas would be most beneficial for all of us. There were greater opportunities for our son and myself.

As I predicted, Craig had met Lonna and was moving in with her. Lonna lived in one of the best school districts in the city, if not the state. I couldn't have dreamed of a more perfect match for him; he and Lonna had more in common than we did, and she adored him. She had two older sons, so it was nice to think of our son one day having siblings that I didn't have to bear. Things were coming together nicely and cordially among all of us, but I was beginning to stress about my new responsibilities, and having to learn technology that I never bothered to learn before.

Craig took care of the bills, mortgage, insurance, taxes, and anything to do with the internet for the past seventeen years. I realized I was a victim of the stay-at-home-mom syndrome, when a woman dedicates most of her career establishing years to home and family. I lived in a bubble of my own choosing, and alienated myself from the evolving world of technology. I busied myself with being great at cooking, cleaning, decorating, and throwing fabulous theme parties during the holidays for family and friends. I focused on being an attentive mom, playing with my son, attending all school activities, and making sure he would grow up confident and loved. Although this is an honorable and important job and purpose in life, I was naïve to put all my eggs in one basket. I was dependent on Craig for more than financial support and it was time for me to learn how to survive on my own.

I was so thankful I had a patient and cooperative soon to be ex-husband. He and Lonna were in no hurry for us to get a divorce. They were both understanding that I still needed to be on his company insurance, and he had to cosign on my house loan. He wanted me to pursue a career I would enjoy, and have the time to grow my income.

He did not want me to struggle or stress and for that I am lucky and grateful.

It was time to hang up my apron and venture out into the working world, and even time to think about dating again as well. I had been away from Dallas for eight years and didn't keep in touch with any old friends. I had not been in the dating world for twenty years. I heard about internet dating on a commercial one night and thought maybe I should give it a try. It would give me some computer experience and might be fun on my lonely weekend nights when my son was with his Dad.

I was looking forward to engaging in some flirtatious encounters and a few dates for fun. I thought I was a fairly good looking woman. I took care of my face and body. I used skin care, and I ran three to five miles every day. Internet dating would push me out of my comfort zone, and I was ready to cast a line and see who was biting.

One early Sunday evening I settled in on my bed with my laptop. I pulled up the Match.com site and clicked on the *search for free* tab. The little window came up where you put in your ZIP Code, and how many miles you want to search. I have always enjoyed being a big fish in a little pond so I decided to enter ten miles. After a few seconds, pages of available men in the pond I chose were viewable in the privacy of my own room. This was pretty cool. It was catalog shopping for men. I saw one that interested me so I clicked on the picture. Another window popped up. In order to see more pictures of him or read about his likes and wants I had to subscribe, fill my own profile, upload pictures, and pay $19.95 per month.

I knew there would be a catch. The internet dating site baited their hook with the search for free tab. I took the bait. I thought if I'm going to do this dating thing I might as well commit to three months. I figured it's sort of like fishing, a sport that requires patience, and drinking. I poured myself a glass of red wine, and typed in my credit card information. The grueling part of the process was upon me, describing myself and what I was looking for in a mate. Ugh!

The first thing I had to come up with was a name. The name was supposed to be a catchy title instead of my real name. Some of the men's names where quite revealing of what they were looking for, one of them was "Swinger4two." Wow, that was bold. At least he knows

what he wants. I wanted my title to be a part of my name, Joy something, catchy and maybe a little sexy. I narrowed it down to three:
Joyofmine
JoyousProcess
Joy-Time

I went with JoyousProcess. This was definitely a process and I was hopeful that it would be joyous. Next I had to come up with a tag line or quote, something clever insinuating my purpose for being on the dating site. I sat there for about thirty minutes really contemplating why I was doing this right now. I wasn't even divorced yet, and might not be for up to a year. I was raised Catholic and everything I was doing and thinking was wrong according to the Catholic faith. I wasn't trying to save my marriage, in fact, I basically threw him onto another woman's hook. I was probably going to be held responsible for Craig's infidelity at the pearly gates. To top it off I am looking to date another man before I am divorced. I am for sure going to hell for all of this, but I wanted some fun in my life, so there it was, my tag line, something to do with FUN.

"Catch One for Fun." I knew this might get me in trouble and probably hook me some Catfish, but I didn't want to jump into another serious long term relationship. I wanted to throw caution to the wind and be twenty again. I had enough responsibilities piled on my plate and dating for fun was going to be my outlet, or rather my distraction. I wanted to keep it simple and fun, no strategy or preconceived idea. I was not searching for my forever dude like my sister Tara who had been divorced for four years.

She had moved in with me while she waited to close on the house she was buying down the street. We were supporting each other in our new adventure of being over forty and dating again. She read somewhere to make a list of all the characteristics you want in a mate and all the ones you don't want. She had her list and was sticking to it this time in her dating expedition. I wasn't in the same boat; she was looking for her king fish, I was looking for a fun fish. So my list was something like this:

1) FUN
2) PASSIONATE (about anything and everything)
3) OUTGOING (exciting and energetic, has stories to tell)

4) SEXY (muscular arms and chest)

This was all I wanted in a potential date for now, my list could change and probably would eventually when I was ready for something more serious.

It was time to fill out my profile.

I am forty-two and separated. I have an eleven year old son.

I am 5'9'' tall and weigh about 150 pounds give or take depending on the season.

I have long wavy light brown hair and blue eyes.

I am athletic with a curvy feminine shape.

I enjoy playing golf about once per month, and I run for exercise daily. When traveling I like to hike, snorkel, and site see.

My favorite food is Mexican. Love margaritas on a patio, that makes me feel as if I were in Mexico.

I enjoy going to sporting events and sometimes watch them on television. I like music concerts and small venues.

I love to dance, except Country and Western.

I used to be a singer in a rock band so I like all kinds of music and am always open to listen to new artists that are eclectic and not always mainstream.

I read and take in a movie occasionally, but much of my free time is spent outside. Throwing the football and shooting hoops with my son are a few of my favorite pastimes. Grilling out in the back yard and having a couple glasses of wine at the end of the day is part of my routine. To dress up, and go out on the town is nice every now and then.

I was raised Catholic and although no longer practicing, I consider myself spiritual in my everyday life.

Income: Tell you later.

Now, what kind of man I am looking for:

Age: 42-52

Height: 6'-6'5" I'm a tall girl. I like to wear high heels occasionally. I prefer my man to be taller than me, but it's not a deal breaker. If he is confident and can hold his own, then 5'10" is acceptable.

Hair color: I like dark haired men but I'm starting to have a thing for the salt and pepper look and even that silver fox color. I prefer a full head of hair, but if a man is losing his hair I would rather he be bald.

Eye color: I have no preference on eye color as long as they have them, or at least one with an eye patch. The pirate look could be interesting, a little Johnny Depp action.
Body type: According to my want list, a muscular chest and arms. I suppose I should be specific and ask for the rest of the body as well.
I would like someone who enjoys playing golf and exercises regularly. Has a love for music and dancing. Reads and likes movies.
Travels for vacation at least once per year, and spends a good portion of their free time outside.
I want someone who has a cocktail or beer or wine occasionally but no binge drinkers.
I prefer someone who is spiritual. It is important to me to be with someone who believes in a higher power. I don't judge anyone who doesn't believe, but it is an important commonality for me.
Income: I put 50k-100k not because I want someone to spend money on me or support me, just so we can afford to have fun.
I am looking for a great kisser but everyone has a different perspective on what a good kisser is, I'll have to play that one by lips.

I was feeling pretty good about my progress up to now. There it was, the picture upload. I dreaded this part, not only because it is so difficult picking the right pictures to portray yourself in a fabulous light, but I struggled with the technical aspect of it. I was still pretty tech-challenged. Before moving back to Dallas my extent of computer use was looking up homes on Realtor.com. Craig did all the techy stuff and my son was more than capable, but I felt it inappropriate to have my eleven year old son upload a bikini shot onto my Match profile. I was frustrated after an hour of trying to get pictures that Craig had downloaded from my camera to my computer onto the Match profile section. I was about to give up and shut it down when the doorbell rang. I jumped up and ran to the door.

"Hey Craig, how's it going?" I sighed as I closed the door behind him.

"I'm good. What's up with you? You look a bit stressed." He stood like a statue in the entry way. It is so strange how you could live with a man for seventeen years, give birth to his kid in front of him and as soon as you become estranged there's an unnerving unfamiliarity. When I was a little girl my Dad would pick me up from my mom's house. He wouldn't even come inside, instead he waited outside at the curb by his truck. My slight discomfort with Craig wasn't bad in comparison. We were quite easy going around each other and I was good with his new girlfriend too, we were definitely the exception to the rule.

"Do you think you could help me with something? I'm trying to upload some pictures to this internet dating site and you know me, I can't figure it out. If I don't put any pictures up then no one will take my bait."

"What site are you on? And what is bait?"

"Oh I'm on Match.com, and bait is what I call all the stuff they ask you to fill out on the sites to catch someone. I'm sort of thinking of this whole process as a fishing expedition." Craig shook his head and chuckled.

I started to head back to my room. "Are you coming?"

"Oh you want me to come back there?"

"Yes, my computer is back here." I knew he had something churning in his head though he rarely voiced it, he was the quiet type. I often wondered what was going on in his head all through our marriage. He was very intelligent and read all kinds of literature. He was strong, and emotionally stable, much more than I was. I was outgoing and wanted to be a star, the life of the party. He was musically talented and mysterious which is what attracted me to him, and it didn't hurt that he was tall, dark, and handsome. He had long wavy black hair, big blue eyes, and looked amazing in a double breasted European suit. He was in the computer business when I met him. I was lucky to marry him and have his child.

I could always count on him for support and help in anything I wanted to do, he supported me when I went back to college, and helped me type my papers on the computer from my hand written notes. Now we were separated and he's uploading my pictures to a dating site so I can catch a date with another man. He went into the pictures on my computer, grabbed a nice face picture, a full body picture of me in shorts and a T-shirt, and a formal black dress picture from a wedding I went to a month prior to moving to Dallas. He hit the enter key and said, "Done. You are live on Match.com!"

We walked back to the entryway. Our son was packed for a two week stay with his Dad for the summer. He was excited to meet

Lonna's two sons for the first time. I hugged him goodbye, and they headed out to the car.

"Hey Joy, be careful…tell your mom or sister when you do go out to meet someone. There can be some crazies on those dating sites."

"Yes of course…I wasn't born yesterday." I closed the door and as I leaned against it, a surge of fear and regret flooded my brain. I suddenly felt very alone and naïve. The dating world was so different than I remembered. We didn't have emailing and texting. I started to wonder if I would be any good at these forms of communication. I feared much would get lost in translation for me. I am more animated with my facial expressions and tone. I had to start somewhere in this new age of dating. I was thankful to be starting out looking to catch one for fun… and not THE ONE.

CHAPTER TWO
CATCH ONE FOR FUN

After searching for about an hour on Match for someone worth casting a line to, I decided to take a break. I was a bit discouraged with the first five eager beavers who winked as soon as my profile went live. I thought, *if they were really interested, and wanted to be the early bird, why wouldn't they send an email?* A wink was lazy. I took a shower to make myself feel date worthy. I poured a glass of wine and sat down at my computer refreshed and ready to email someone. I was pleased to see while taking my shower I had received two emails.

The first guy's online name was *a surejon 4u.* When I read his profile and saw that he was a surgeon, I thought, *clever.* His email was double spaced and formally written. He assured me he was the perfect height for me at six foot four inches. He mentioned the things we had in common starting with his favorite food, Mexican. He was a leading neurosurgeon in the country, and relayed to me that he didn't have the time to date traditionally which is why he was on the internet dating site. He said between traveling all over the world, and spending time at his beach house in Florida, he wanted to find a companion that would not only be available to travel at any time, but also accepting of his busy work schedule.

The guy looked great on paper or in a *Pretty Woman* movie, but I didn't get the feeling he was what I was looking for. Now, with my focus on a career, I didn't think traveling and being at this man's beck and call was conducive to what I was trying to accomplish.

I clicked on the second email; "OOOLALA!" I yelled for Tara to come see the guy seducing me from the computer screen. She skipped into the living room and looked over my shoulder as I scrolled through his pictures.

"Wow, he's more my type than yours, you should give him to me." My sister had been dating a past boyfriend and a guy she met on her flight home from New York. The long distance relationship wasn't working out and neither was the past boyfriend, who could only commit to an occasional lunch. We sat there drooling over one of this guy's pictures where he was standing with his golf buddies. They were each holding a driver golf club. I realized I was blushing as a warmth came over me while enjoying the vision of him in his picture. It felt good to know I could still be aroused. He was about average height with a perfectly proportioned physique. His thick silver hair glimmered in the sunlight. I was physically attracted to him from his pictures, but I wanted to see if we had anything in common besides golf and our taste in music.

He liked golf, skiing, scuba diving, going to music concerts, and sporting events; mostly baseball and college football. I wasn't a big baseball fan, but if I could sit and hold on to his biceps, I could be entertained for nine innings. Although he was vague about his profession, income, life's purpose, ambitions and wants, I was intrigued. His tag line read: I'm ready for what's next. I figured we were probably a good match for now…at least for having fun. My heart beat faster and my palms were sweating as I sat there thinking about something clever to say in my email back to him.

I wrote: *I love your golf picture. I appreciate your vague profile, more for me to find out when we meet. Hint! Hint!* He immediately emailed me back wanting to meet me as well, but would have his kids all week, so we'd have to wait until the following Monday. My heart sank for a moment, but then I remembered I was going to help Tara move into her new home that weekend. I wrote back with that would be fine, and gave him my real name and number. I was excited for our first date. I wasn't interested in meeting anyone else before I met him, so I tried to stay off of the dating site. I answered a couple of emails but didn't commit to any other dates.

On Saturday, my sister and I were moving all her stuff from my house and her storage unit into her new home. We had just finished the last load, and I popped the cork of a bottle of champagne to celebrate. My cell phone rang. It was Dave, the guy from Match whom I was anxiously waiting to meet. I suddenly had butterflies in my stomach, and all the blood rushed to my face. "Hi Joy. It seems I am now available this weekend. I know its short notice, but can you go out tonight?" I looked over at my sister filling two red solo cups with champagne, and realized I was going to ditch her for a guy I hadn't actually met yet. I looked at my watch; it was seven o'clock and I was a filthy mess.

"I could meet you around nine, is that too late?"

"That sounds great. Where is a good place to meet near you?"

"Well, I just finished helping my sister move, so I'd like to go somewhere casual. How about meeting at this little neighborhood bar down the street from me called, Scruffy's?"

"Okay, I'll see you at nine at Scruffy's. Should I shave?" He asked and chuckled. I laughed along with him.

"Cute. I'll see you soon." I already liked his sense of humor and he had a nice voice. I gulped down the champagne in my cup, and begged my sister to forgive me for deserting her. She waved me off, sipping champagne from her solo cup and looking around the living room at all the boxes to unpack. She was fine with me leaving as she was the type who would have the house looking like she had lived there for a year a day later.

I hurried back to my house to get ready. I was nervous and a little tipsy from the champagne. I did the three Ss to get ready-showered, shaved and scrunched my hair while it air dried. I put some eyeliner and mascara on to showcase my blue eyes, a little bronzer for my cheeks, and finished with a frosted lip gloss. After throwing on a pair of faded blue jeans and a black V-neck fitted shirt, I slipped on my wedge-heeled sandals and was out the door.

I arrived on time and sat in the parking lot for about three minutes when my phone tweeted, "pulling in now." A black Mercedes slipped in beside my black Lexus. I sat there for a second, watching to see him get out of his car. He emerged wearing faded jeans that fit him slightly loose but shaped his bottom just right. He wore a form-fitting, white, short sleeved shirt that showed off his tan biceps. I got out of my car and made my way around to where he was standing.

He looked directly into my eyes and smiled, "I'm Dave… and you must be…a Joy?" I smirked at his Freudian slip.

"I am Joy, and we'll see… It's nice to meet you Dave."

We exchanged a flirty glance and I grabbed his arm just under his bicep. We started walking toward the entrance. He had a swagger to his walk, and I felt a contagious energy while I held onto him. He smelled clean and fresh, no heavy cologne.

We slipped into a little corner booth next to the bar. He was clean shaven but had a rugged face, like a combination of Richard Gere and Robert Redford. His eyes twinkled even in the dim lighting. Dave ordered a vodka and soda with a lemon and I ordered a glass of red wine. We both looked at each other and smiled after the waitress left to get our drinks. After we covered the ice-breaker formalities, such as what's your favorite color, and do you prefer beach trips to ski trips, I relaxed into the tales he told of his upbringing. Even though he grew up in the Midwest and I in Texas, we both came from a large family of women, and we were both the baby of the family. Like I was, he was usually the center of attention and people were drawn to him because of his outgoing personality, igniting fun and excitement. When he moved away from his small home town to attend college at Texas A&M, and then ended up in Dallas, we discovered we had both worked and frequented the same bars and dance clubs in the early nineties. We listened to a lot of the same music, past and current. Throughout the first hours of our date, I thought we were a close match and I was having a blast.

The bartender announced last call. I didn't want the night to end. Dave paid the tab and asked, "Do you want to go somewhere else?"

"Yes please!" I scooched out of the booth and as I turned to walk ahead of him, he placed his hand on the small of my back. I felt a tantalizing tingle up my spine.

"Are you okay with me driving to the next place? I'll bring you back. I promise."

"Sure." He opened the car door and closed it behind me.

"This is a nice car. I don't think I've ever been in a Benz."

"This is no ordinary Benz, this is an AMG. This car is fast!"

I had always heard about guys and their relationship with fast cars, but I had never dated any of them. I dated guys that drove trucks or jeeps. When Dave spoke of his car, his eyes lit up as if he was describing a lover. His excitement was contagious as he sped through a yellow light, going sixty-five in a forty mph speed zone.

If this guy is as passionate about being with his woman as he is with his car, I'm in for a treat someday.

We made it safely to Kenny's, a quaint establishment that reminded me of a bar in Manhattan or Boston with its dim lighting and rich dark wood interior. We sat at the bar, facing each other. I placed both of my hands on his knees and asked, "What was it in my profile that made you send me an email?"

"Everything really, your long curly hair, your big blue eyes, and your smile was what made me start typing the email. I have to be honest, I'm sure what you had to say in your profile was thought provoking, but I emailed you purely on physical attraction. But now that I've met you, I'm really enjoying all of you." I had forgotten what it felt like when my body reacted to another. The exchange of energy and emotion was palpable; I felt a moist glistening forming above my brow and at the back of my neck. *Could it be the wine, the chemistry, or a hot flash?*

My sister had hot flashes when she was stressed and unhappy. I was not stressed, I was happy at this particular moment, so it must have been the wine or most likely my fancying Dave.

"Well I am thoroughly enjoying all of you as well. Is it hot in here?" I blotted my forehead with my napkin and I thought, *Oh I'm sure that was attractive, he probably thinks he's out with a lady going through the change.*

"No I think its twenty degrees hotter just between me and you." He winked and then finished paying the tab.

We walked back to his car and before opening my door he leaned me against it and kissed me. His lips were made for mine and his tongue was ever so polite for this first kiss. My knees began to buckle. He reached around my waist to support me while holding the rhythm of the kiss. Our lips parted and I took a deep breath and closed my eyes so to never forget the moment. He stood holding me and when I opened my eyes he looked into them and asked, "You okay?"

"Yes, I'm good, really good. Thank you…for that…kiss. It's been a really long time." I turned to get in the car.

Before he closed my door he asked, "So how long?"

"Years" I admitted as he closed the door. He ran to his side and jumped in the car.

"What? Did you say years?"

"Yes."

"How can that be? You aren't even divorced - you're separated?"

"My husband and I had actually separated a couple of years ago. It just took a while to sell our house before moving back to Dallas."

"I don't believe you. That's impossible, that's insane! You are saying I am the first guy you have kissed in years? There's no way." He was shaking his head as he drove me back to my car.

"Look it's a long story, and one day you may want to hear it, but for now I would very much like to enjoy another kiss please." We had just pulled up to my car in Scruffy's parking lot, now empty. He jumped out, opened my door, and pulled me up into his arms and kissed me like before, but with more intensity. I could feel a tingling all over, a yearning I had not felt in over a decade. I so desperately wanted him to come home with me. *Oh my! I am in so much trouble with this one.* We stood there in the warm summer breeze making out for thirty minutes. I didn't want to let him go, but it was almost two in the morning. He put me in my car and leaned in for one more kiss.

"I would like to see you again. How about lunch on Monday?"

How about breakfast? "Lunch on Monday is perfect."

He tapped the hood of my car and swaggered off to his.

Sunday seemed like seven days rather than one. I looked at the Match winks and emails I had received just to pass the time. I wasn't interested in anyone but Dave. My mind kept rambling. *What if he is still looking at, and emailing other women? I hope not, but I'm on it, so why wouldn't he be on it? It was one date, and I'm not even divorced yet. Even if I wanted, I can't really pursue a relationship with him, but WOW I'm so hot for him.* I had to get out of my head, so I could be pleasant and normal on our lunch date Monday. I didn't want to seem jealous and crazy so soon or he'd go racing off in that fast car of his, leaving me in his rearview mirror. Instead I thought about what to wear, and if I should straighten my hair this time. The phone rang and it was Dave. I felt like a school girl with a crush on the guy I never thought would call me.

"Hey Joy, I'm calling to confirm our lunch date, and wanted to know if you would like to come out to my home in Plano. I can grill for us, and we can eat by the pool. It's supposed to be beautiful out. You can even bring your bikini and lay out while I cook if you like."

It took me about a second to answer, "Yes, that sounds fun." *I must be crazy I don't even know this man, and I'm going to his home to lay out by his pool in a bikini.*

I don't know why, but everything in my being said it was fine and I was safe with him. There was nothing in my head or gut telling me I should be worried for my safety, and I definitely wasn't worried for my virtue. That was taken a long time ago, by the one I thought was my soul mate. Dave reminded me a lot of Mark, my first love. They didn't look anything alike but the feeling I felt around both of them was similar. My feelings were intense. I wanted to be with him all the time, and if I wasn't with him I was thinking about him.

I arrived at Dave's home in Plano, a suburb about ten miles north of my house. He had a single story traditional style home which he had remodeled beautifully with a Mediterranean look. The front exterior was enticing, with a stone-laid path leading into an enclosed courtyard. Once inside the courtyard, there were showcased glass double doors, protected with ornate, gray wrought iron. Before I could ring the door bell, Dave appeared. Opening both doors as if on the "Life Styles of the Rich and Famous" he smiled and left them wide open, as I stepped inside onto the travertine floors which ran throughout. He pulled me in for a hug, and grabbed the bag I had packed with my bikini and pool towel. Once he released me from his magnetic embrace, I gasped at the floor to ceiling windows that beckoned me to the pool and three sheet waterfalls cascading from a travertine wall. Dave walked me through the rest of the house, ending the tour with the master bedroom. His home was nothing like a bachelor pad. Every room was painted with designer colors, accessorized with pillows, paintings, and floral arrangements bursting from floor urns and center pieces. A crystal chandelier over the modern multi-stained dark and light wood table inspired fabulous dinner parties.

"You can change into your suit in here." He closed the door. I stepped into the master bathroom and marveled at the huge bathtub, envisioning the luxury of soaking in it every night. His house was clean, without clutter, almost as if it were practically staged. *So my style. I lived seventeen years with someone who never threw anything away. I preferred to purge things at least twice per year. Oops, I better hurry up or he might think I'm going through all his personals and bank statements.* I put on my white string bikini and walked back through the living room to the kitchen. Dave was standing at the counter with his back to me, preparing what I assumed was our lunch.

"Hey is there anything I can help with?" I asked hoping I didn't startle him. He immediately turned around, and made a quick glance up and down. He smiled and walked over to me. Placing his arms around my waist and letting his hands subtly rest just over my bottom, he kissed me, and pressed himself against me just slightly. I could tell he was happy I was there.

He backed away and said, "I have a pork tenderloin marinating."

"I can see that." I playfully proclaimed.

"You are bad, but I like it. Hey let's go get some sun."

He grabbed my hand and led me out to the pool. I toe-tested the temperature of the water, pleased to find it warm. I slipped all the way in from the side of the pool. I waded over to one of the sheet waterfalls, and dunked myself under the water. The water ran over my face and hair as Dave came up, pulled me close and kissed my wet lips, making his way down my neck. His mouth was silky and smooth, with slow rhythmic caresses on my skin. We played in the waterfalls letting the pressured water massage our backs and necks. The water temperature seemed to reach new heights with us in the pool.

"Okay we have to get out, I've got to feed us before we…you know…"

"Pass out from hunger?" I asked coyly.

"Yes, exactly." He jumped out of the pool, his tan hairless body glistening in the sun.

Dave grilled up the pork tenderloin and put it over salad. We spent three hours talking, laughing, and listening to some of his favorite poolside set lists. Our time together was effortless and way too short. Again I didn't want our date to end, but I had to leave and go pick up Dawson at his Dad's house. I knew it would be torture till I would see him again.

CHAPTER THREE
STINK BAIT

It was Wednesday evening, I was sitting quietly in my living room starring out at the golf course. I was trying hard not to take it personally that I had not heard from Dave since our fantastic lunch date on Monday. I had a gut-wrenching feeling something was wrong, and I had no idea how to get off the crazy train in my head. *Had I freaked him out telling him how long it had been since I had been kissed or intimate with a man? Maybe he didn't really like how I kissed? What if he was one of those guys just looking to have fun, the date-as-many-as-he-can, adding another to his brag belt and had no intentions of seeing me again? Oh God, I hope not, I actually liked him. Oh shit, I pray this doesn't turn out to be like a high school crush. Okay Joy, you have to approach this dating thing in your forties with less drama.* The anxiety I was feeling over Dave, drudged up the memories of my first love.

At the age of fifteen, I was the singer of a rock band, or rather a garage band, and our first gig was the opening act for another band at a high school dance. I had just finished singing my last song. Back stage the guitar player for the other band, Mark, was slipping into his tight leather pants when I walked in on him.

"Oops sorry!" I said as I turned to leave when I saw his bare bottom.

"No, don't go, stay." he said. I felt butterflies in the pit of my stomach and a fluttering between my legs. It wasn't that he was great looking, but his confidence lured me back into the room to see more of him and hear what he had to say. He had long dark hair and full pouty lips, fair skin and quite the muscular build for a rock-n-roll musician. He finished pulling his pants up and walked toward me. "You've got a really good voice, you should consider joining our band. Can you sing backup?" He asked.

"I'm a lead singer."

"I know, but can you sing background vocals?"

"I'm sure I could. But I haven't had to. Hey I haven't even heard your band play yet, so I don't know if I'd want to join your band."

He looked at me and grinned with a twinkle in his eye and said, "Who's opening for who? See you in a bit." He grabbed his black electric guitar and went up the back stairs onto the stage.

When his band finished playing their first set, I was impressed by the difficulty of the songs they played and played well. I couldn't help but dream of going further with them as my band, not to mention the attraction to Mark. *After I joined the band I'd be their lead singer, and he'd be my guitar player, and my boyfriend.* I knew he had a girlfriend, she was at the sound check earlier that day, but how serious could they be, he wasn't much older than me. He strutted off the stage, "Well, are you joining us or not?" He brushed the side of my cheek with his hand as he passed by me to grab some water and a towel.

"Um, Yes I would like to join your band, but I want to sing lead on at least half the set list." He winked at me and said, "Of course you will. I'll pick you up Tuesday at 4:30 for your first rehearsal with us."

When I arrived home from school that Tuesday, I scrambled around looking for my cut off denim shorts and a white T-shirt to wear to rehearsal. I was more nervous about being in the car alone with Mark than singing with the band for the first time. Mark picked me up in a small, rusty two-door 1976 Chevette. He put his hand on my seat touching my bare thigh as I got in. He looked over at me with his light brown eyes and said, "Oh sorry I always rest my hand there…it's a habit, you don't mind do you?"

"No, if you don't mind making me the lead singer of the band." I smiled and looked straight ahead. I felt a tingle between my legs giving me goosebumps all over.

He glanced down at my legs and saw the effect he had on me. "Sure I won't mind backing you up," he laughed, put his car in first and sped off.

Over the following three weeks of rehearsals, the sexual tension building between Mark and I was hard to ignore, I was falling for him and I couldn't stop thinking about what would eventually happen. I wanted him to be my boyfriend, and although he had a girlfriend it didn't stop me from planning our future together in my head. *We would be in a band together, become famous in the music business, be madly in love, travel the world on tour, and when we were ready, we would settle down, and maybe have a kid or two.* For the time, I had to play it cool and act like I was just in the band for the music and focus on our upcoming gig.

Our band was scheduled to play at our high school senior's graduation party. We had a two hour set list with cover songs from the bands U2, The Police, Rush, Pat Benatar, Heart, Missing Persons, and Led Zeppelin just to name a few. Mark was taking me home after our last rehearsal before the gig. It was an early summer evening with a warm breeze and a clear sky. He walked me to my front door. He turned me around and held my face in his hands and kissed me gently but deeply. The breeze swept over me and his kiss transcended me into a place I had never known. I had kissed a few boys before, but never felt what was happening to me at that moment. I felt every cell in my body awaken. He left me with all kinds of emotions swirling throughout my mind and body, and I found it hard to get a good night sleep.

So many of the graduates couldn't believe how good the band was. As I talked with some of them afterward, Mark pulled me away and asked, "Can you come over to my house and spend the day with me tomorrow, without the band?"

"Why? Did you finally realize I should be singing lead on everything and you want to help me learn all of your songs now?" I lightly punched him in the shoulder and laughed.

"No. Carol and I broke up yesterday because I want to be with you."

I felt my heart leap and my mouth curve into the biggest grin, I could hardly contain myself. "Sure, but how will I get there? Didn't your car break down on the way out here tonight?"

"Yes. Do you think your sister could bring you around lunch?"

"Yes, I'll be there." I said as I walked toward my mom, who was waiting to take me home. The whole way home I was going crazy with excitement, I was finally getting what I wanted, but I was also a nervous wreck. All these months we had just been flirting, I hadn't thought about what would happen if our relationship became real. I had never been all the way with a guy, he had been with Carol for two years, and I knew they had.

The next day, my sister dropped me off at his house. He was outside, waiting for me. He took my hand, and we started walking. We walked through a heavily wooded area along a creek. The trees and brush made it very private, like a world away from the city. He motioned for me to get on his back and carried me through the water to the other side, where there was a sheltered, grassy cove. We sat down and he started kissing me very softly, then gently eased me back onto the soft grass. As his kisses became more intense, my head was spinning. All I could think of was the deal I had made with myself, of waiting for just the right person, maybe even until I got married, wasn't going to stick. *I certainly wasn't getting married anytime soon, so he must be the right person, he was it, my first love.* When we left this magical place I couldn't stop smiling and I didn't feel the shame or guilt like I thought I would. I went home in love, and thought my world was the most amazing place to live.

Two days later, I wanted to die. He called, informing me his x-girlfriend was pregnant. Mark had been adopted and he felt he needed to marry her and support her and the baby. I put the phone down. Chills ran through my body and a physical sickness took over. I ran to the bathroom and threw up. I felt all the blood pool in the bottom of my stomach. I couldn't hear anything, not even my own voice in my head. Everything was still and muted, a nothingness took over. I felt like the very essence of my soul had been sucked right out of me and there was no purpose left in life. I didn't care about anything or anyone at that moment.

Once the initial physical sickness wore off, I couldn't stop crying for months. I remained in a six month depression, only going to school, and then sitting in my room listening to Pink Floyd. Sitting in my living room twenty-seven years later remembering the feelings of hope-lessness and regret I prayed I wouldn't have to experience it all over again with Dave.

After my journey through the past, I turned back to the future, and checked my Match account. If Dave didn't call, at least I could scan the plethora of men to distract me from how awful I was feeling. Hopefully I'd find one to trump Dave. I was settling in for a long night. I had just poured a glass of wine when my phone rang. It was Dave. My heart raced and the blood rushed to my head, my hands shaking as I answered the phone.

"Hey Joy, I'm sorry for not calling you sooner but I…I've been thinking a lot about how you are only separated and you haven't even filed for the divorce yet…that's a little unsettling for me and I don't think we should keep seeing each other…Joy…Are you there?"

"Um, yes. Yes I'm here. You knew I was separated from my profile, and we even talked about it on our first date. Why did you want a second date if you had such a problem with it? And why did you allow us to take it to a physical level?"

"I know. I'll be honest with you, when I saw your pictures and your tag line, catch one for fun, well, you looked fun and I thought it wouldn't hurt to meet. I didn't expect to really like you. I know that sounds bad, but I've been on a few of these internet dating things, and I haven't really met anyone I liked seriously, it was just something to pass the time, and get me out of the house once in a while. After we met, I knew I liked you more than a friend. I thought I'd give it a shot with us, but then you told me you haven't even filed for divorce yet. I saw that as a red flag. I'm sorry."

"I'm sorry too. So I wonder why the dating sites even allow a status of separated? Do you think it is mainly for other separated individuals, or is it for those who aren't looking for commitment but rather a good time?"

"I don't know, but I hope you don't think that about me. I like you, I've just had a bad experience with a woman who said she was separated and she wasn't. She was still very married, and her husband found out, and came over to kick my ass one night. I just can't have that kind of drama. I have kids to think about."

"Okay, I get that, but you have sought out women that were separated before, why?"

"I think it's because where I am in my life with my kids, they're still young and need my support and guidance, but it gets complicated with my x-wife, so I try to keep my social life pretty simple."

"At any point of our date the other day when it was getting a bit hot in your pool, did you know you felt this way about me, not being divorced?"

"Yes, I'm sorry about that, but like I said, I really like you and looking back I wished I would have stopped us. It took me a couple of days to figure out how wrong I was for moving forward with you, and not being honest about what had happened to me before. Honestly, I wish you were divorced."

"So is the red flag that I am still married, or that I haven't filed for the divorce yet?"

"I guess both."

"So when I am divorced, I hope we meet again Dave. Goodbye for now."

"Me too Joy…goodbye for now."

I hung up the phone as the tears and the wails poured out of me. It felt like my first love heart break all over again. I had no business being on a dating site. It's no wonder I caught one that had a little fun with me and then threw me back. I realized just wanting someone for fun wasn't how I had pictured it in my mind. Being separated and on an internet dating site gave the impression I can't commit to a marriage or a divorce.

The next morning, I called Craig and told him I wanted to file for the divorce. Craig always wanted to help in any way he could, but he thought I should wait until I was more financially set. Once he realized it was something I was set on doing in order to move forward with my life, he said for me to pick out an attorney that would mediate our divorce. I scheduled a meeting with an attorney, while Craig and I worked out all the details of the divorce on a legal pad. Two weeks later, I sat across from the attorney, handed him the legal pad with our specifications, and said, "Let's get it done."

He looked at the pad, and then looked at me and said, "Okay. I'll get this filed and it should be final in a couple of months."

The day had been long and draining, but I was feeling good about getting my divorce filed. I sat there in my room watching an episode of *The Bachelor*. I didn't really want to get back on the dating site until my divorce was final. I started to wonder if internet dating could turn into an addiction for some people. *Hell, I was afraid it already had for me, twice I sought comfort in scrolling through the pictures of men, thinking maybe there was one that would make all my dreams come true. It was my new escape from reality, one that was so convenient, but distracting from the things I should be focusing on, like my career.*

I pulled up my account and checked my inbox. There were two emails and a few winks. I was more interested in the actual profile than the pictures this time, paying attention to what they wrote. I needed to read between the lines to better understand what kind of person they were and why they were on the dating site. I was starting to see some commonality in what most men were looking for, or rather not looking for in a woman. One of them wrote: *looking for someone that goes with the flow and isn't high maintenance*. Another one: *looking for a woman who likes to watch sports or doesn't mind if I do.*

While trying to decide if I wanted to respond to the two emails I had received, I was feeling a little gun shy, but I figured what's the hurt in meeting a few new friends? I have always believed single men and women can't be just friends because there is always one who wants more. Against my better judgment, I checked out the two emails, and found both of them to be somewhat attractive with interesting profiles. The first one had the Mr. Clean look, big and bald. He was seven years my senior, a video and short film producer, and had been divorced for seven years.

I decided to respond to Mr. Clean. I thanked him for liking my pics and showing interest in me, and I'd be up for meeting him soon. The second guy that emailed me was a clean-cut business man with pictures of him participating in triathlons and charity events. In good shape and involved with community is a good combination; I had always wanted to participate in a race for a cause and other charitable works. I emailed him back and said I'd be interested in meeting soon. I kept my emails short and to the point for fear of giving off the wrong signals.

I received an email back Thursday afternoon from Dan, the Mr. Clean guy. He said he was going out of town with family for a wedding, but we could text and talk while he drove down to Austin. I was hesitant to give him my number so soon, so I emailed him back and asked when he was leaving and if we could start with a few emails to get to know each other better before I gave him my number. He emailed back with "LMAO."

"What does that mean?"

He typed back, "*Laughing my ass off* and what rock have you been under?"

I was a little put off by his sarcasm, however I was a bit naïve and uninformed with texting lingo. I gradually adapted to his abrupt sense of humor and decided to give him my number so we could talk over the weekend.

We spoke on the phone during his three and half hour drive from Dallas to Austin. Speaking mostly about his kids who were all in their late high school and college years, I felt more at ease, thinking he must be a decent guy if he was so dedicated to his kids. Professionally, he was working on a new project, which he wanted me to come by the shoot on Monday for our first date. The weekend came and went and he called me on his way home to remind me of our date at the studio in Deep Ellum.

When I pulled up to the urban, single story, brick building a surge of creative excitement filled me and for a moment, I was back in my twenties when Craig and I recorded the songs we wrote together in a studio similar to this one. As I walked in, there was no one at the reception desk or in the two long hallways. There were movie posters, and musical albums framed on the walls. I continued down the far back hall where I heard voices. Peeking into the small window of a studio door, I saw the back of a tall bald man bent over a table looking at a computer screen. I opened the door and squeezed into the room quietly. Standing in one corner was a thin man and a woman having their naked bodies painted.

I was about to slip back out the door before anyone noticed. Dan turned around and pointed at me, "You must be Joy." He rushed over and gave me a big hug. My five foot nine inch frame was swallowed up by his massive arms. I felt my neck might break pinned between his chest and shoulder. He was handsome in a barbaric kind of way. He spun around to instruct everyone on what needed to get done in the amount of time they had the studio booked, and then he said he was stepping out for a bit.

We walked down the hall and snuck into a sound proof recording studio. When the door shut behind him he scooped me up and threw me over his shoulder like a sack of potatoes. I screamed and then laughed. I had never had a man do this to me, and I just remembered during one of our conversations on the phone, I had told him I had always dated guys that were not exactly big enough to ever pick me up. He set me down gently on a long yellow leather sofa, provided for musicians when they were recording long hours. The lights were dimmed and it was sort of romantic, but I hardly knew this man. I was a little uncomfortable.

"So you used to be a singer in a band, does this bring back memories?" He plopped down next to me and put his tree trunk of an arm behind me.

"Yes it does, but this studio is much nicer…So what kind of project are you working on in the other room?" I adjusted my position so I could face him.

"We are filming an artistic video of modern dance, color, and eroticism. I guess you could say it's an erotic work of art." He leaned in closer to try and kiss me, I jumped up and paced around the studio to redirect his intentions.

"Would it turn you on to watch something like that?" He asked while tapping his hand on the sofa where I was sitting.

"You know, I think I should probably go, and let you focus on your project."

"What's your hurry and why you so nervous? We've been talking and getting to know each other for the past three days, this is really like our fourth date. I think a fourth date merits a first kiss, don't you?"

"I think you're interesting, but I think you might be moving a bit fast for me."

He stood up and walked toward me. "Let me get this straight, you are separated and on an internet dating site, and you expect me to court you, and treat you like an available woman? Men don't court separated women, they have fun with them because usually that is what the woman is looking for, a reason to get a little strange, test the waters to see what's out there, and then they go back to their husband. That was the impression I got from your profile. Sorry if I misinterpreted." He held out his hand to shake mine. "It was nice meeting you Joy."

I couldn't get out of there fast enough. I felt cheap and tainted, not because of his behavior, although it was distasteful, but because of mine. *Being on an internet dating site before being divorced was like using stink bait.*

CHAPTER FOUR
A NEW SCHOOL

My first few experiences with internet dating helped me to see I was not being true to my heart, instead, I was living through my ego. I justified getting on the dating site because I wanted to be admired and desired again. I felt entitled, seeing Craig had moved on with someone else, not to mention it was easier and more entertaining than figuring out how I was going to be financially independent.

I noticed a pattern with my ego, steering me in any direction away from unfamiliar work and discomfort. While I was married, it seemed I was in an almost constant state of worry, dissatisfaction, entitlement, judgment, and I'll-be-happy-if and when-this happens syndrome. I existed in my marriage by keeping myself busy and exhausted, making it look to myself and others like I was this amazing housewife and mother. While deep inside my heart I knew I wasn't being the person I was meant to be, and I wasn't loving my husband unconditionally.

Once Craig and I actually separated, I was listening to my heart and allowing it to guide me. First, letting go of the comfortable life style I had become accustomed to; living in a big home, going on expensive trips, not worrying about finances, or how my friends and family would perceive me when I wasn't of the higher-income status anymore. I felt authentic with the release of Craig and my comfortable life style. I was open to the possibilities of what living on my own and having a career would bring to my life. Much to my surprise, going out with Dave, having an instant connection with him, and not being legally eligible to be with him, confused my heart and my head.

Looking back on many of my life's decisions, I saw a pattern in how I would choose jobs and relationships requiring the least amount of work with the shortest path to comfort and pleasure. When Dave put a stop to our relationship going any further, it forced me to look at myself. My ego had always been the dominate enforcer, choosing the paths that would get me to the dreams in my head quicker. My heart wanted true love, to be capable of loving someone unconditionally, but I didn't know how or what that really was. Life happened quickly, and the distractions of what my ego wanted would take time away from contemplating and implementing what my heart wanted.

Although I felt my heart being present at times throughout my life, usually in nature, listening to music, singing, dancing, painting, writing, and helping others, it was often vetoed by my head if what my heart wanted required too much thought and discomfort to achieve. For example, pursuing my singing career after I was turned down by the record labels the first time, or if I would have pursued a writing career out of college. Fear of hard work and failure kept me from many things my heart desired, eventually costing me my marriage. I wasn't going to dwell on the should-have and could-haves; I was learning from my mistakes slowly but surely. My date with Dan the video producer left me feeling unprepared. I no longer wanted to take shortcuts to a happy and loving life. I was going to put the hard work in on myself this time, so that I would eventually have and be capable of giving unconditional love in my next relationship.

I didn't think it was important to analyze exactly when my ego had taken over as the CEO of my life, but it was important that I be aware of how and when it could cause drama and distractions from pursuing what my heart wanted. After some time of discernment following Dave, Dan, and filing for my divorce, I came to a clear and focused decision; I would pursue my real estate career first before seeking any new love interest.

The real estate courses were about to begin. It was a fast track 30-day program, and when I passed the state exam I would be a licensed Texas realtor. The program was all day, Monday-Thursday for the entire month of October. It gave me a sense of direction and motivation, knowing by the end of the year I would have a legitimate profession where I would build a career and financial worth on my own.

I pulled into the parking lot of the real estate school, realizing it had been over a decade since I had participated in any formal education. The last school I attended was massage therapy school in 1998. I had been a licensed massage therapist for one year before I gave birth to my son. Practicing massage therapy part time while he was in grade school limited me in building a lucrative business. Attending real estate classes and putting in a typical work day of six to eight hours was practical now that he was in sixth grade.

I walked into a large classroom of long and narrow brown tables placed close together in rows. The conference chairs placed side by side and spaced about two fingers apart meant the eight hours spent sitting in them were not for those with low back issues. I saw there were a few other women beginning their middle-aged careers, who like myself, arrived early. I found a seat at the end of the second to the last row of tables. A gorgeous woman sitting in the last row made eye contact with me. She had long wavy brown hair, dark eyes and high cheek bones. I settled into my seat with my coffee and water bottle on either side of my note paper and pen. I sat there in silence waiting for the class to begin.

Is the beautiful woman behind me in the same boat? Had she married a wonderful man who loved and adored her? Had he supported her financially so she could stay home and raise their kids, making a beautiful home for them? Had he also been supportive of her pursuing a career or project she wanted to start and not finish, but loved that she tried? Had they gone on wonderful vacations or bought vacation homes on a lake or in the hill country? Had her life with this man been perfect in the eyes of all the people who knew them, but she couldn't figure out why she wasn't capable of loving him the way he deserved to be loved? And why she wasn't happy?

While other class members were filing into the classroom taking their seats, I casually nodded hello, but kept on thinking of the life I had recently given up with Craig. I had accepted the role of wife and mother as my calling some fifteen years ago. I remember being proud and content for the first four years with a creative outlet replacing my passion for singing and writing with the remodeling and decorating of our homes. I enjoyed hosting theme parties for family and friends. I kept myself busy with the daily, weekly, monthly, and yearly chores and projects which eventually became my purpose for staying in the marriage. If I went too long without a project, a part of me would get uncomfortable, followed by unhappiness. I would then question the authenticity of our marriage, wondering if my true place on this earth was somewhere else, with someone else, doing something else.

The voices in my head would go back and forth between wanting to work on my marriage or find a way out and start over. I was raised Catholic, so I was taught you did everything you could to stay married even if it meant everyone involved was miserable. No matter what I tried, thought, read, and communicated with Craig, I was never decisive on what I wanted or needed. I dreamed about what it would be like to be single again doing something creative as a career and making my own money. However, when I'd think of pursuing my passion such as singing or writing, a voice convinced me those paths weren't conducive to the life I had accepted as a wife and mother. My other voice would counter, I could pursue those passions while being a wife and mother, but it would be an extreme amount of work. Shortly after entertaining the idea of pursuing a passion of mine, and beginning the work or process, the stronger voice would find all the reasons and excuses why I wouldn't want to do all that extra work. I had it made with my nice house, I didn't have to go to a nine to five job or worry about finances or retirement because I had a great husband that takes care of me, and it was more important I focused on being a good mother. I knew there were people who had both career and family and were successful, happy, and in love with their spouse, but I also fell prey to my ego wanting more time for fun and leisure. The ugly truth of it all, I was lazy when it came to doing work that didn't guarantee success, and interfered with my time for fun and leisure.

I felt guilty of not loving Craig the way he deserved to be loved, wasting years of potential happiness for each of us, including our son. I was stressed and scared for myself and my family. I didn't want Craig or my son to suffer and be unhappy. I had the answers to my conflicting voices in my head, but I didn't know what to do or how to make it right.

Craig and I were no longer sleeping in the same room after seven years of marriage. One night I was sleeping in the guest room at our river house and woke up in a cold sweat. I felt paralyzed by a dream. In the first part of the dream, our home on the river was on fire. I rushed around to find my son. I grabbed him by the wrist and we started running for the hay field out front. There was a crop dusting plane in the field. We got into the plane and I started the engine. After picking up speed, we lifted off the ground and we were flying over the field and the river. My son was standing behind me holding onto my neck. His blue eyes were wide and his hair disheveled. He swallowed hard and said, "Momo, we forgot Daddy." I looked at him, and then I looked behind to see the house explode.

In the second part of the dream there was a lion pacing back and forth in front of me. He swung his paw at me and latched it into my stomach. I looked down and saw my insides pour out onto the ground.

I was an amateur in the study of dreams, but I believed my dreams were like a window into my subconscious and could assist me in working through life's challenges. I wrote the dreams down in my journal knowing they would be explained eventually in time.

After that dream, I went two more years in a constant battle with my inner dialogue over whether to stay in my marriage or get out. I read many self-help and marriage-mending books, I heard Dr. Laura in my head saying that love was a verb, and that I needed to act on it instead of thinking and wishing for it to miraculously be there. All the right words from books and spiritual leaders made sense, and Craig and I attempted different methods for reconnecting and strengthening our relationship, but nothing penetrated my negative mindset. I was in that place of purgatory, where I knew all the right steps to take, yet my ego wouldn't connect with my heart.

One night I woke up with excruciating stomach pain. I thought I was having a heart attack. The dream I had about the lion was a warning, I obviously didn't make the right changes in my life, and it manifested into a physical illness. I knew something had to change.

Shortly after I healed from what turned out to be my dysfunctional gall bladder, we sold the river house. We bought a home in the hill country, giving me a new project, remodeling another home with five acres. The power of distraction from myself seemed to appease me for a few years again. Distractions became my purpose, my purpose became my excuse for not actively loving my husband, and not loving my husband became my guilt. My guilt became fear, and fear of becoming sick again, or dying young like my brother did finally gave me the courage to make a real change and separate from Craig.

Thanks to Craig for being a stable and caring man, our separation was cordial. He was in a new relationship soon after, somehow making it easier on us both. I was very happy for him and felt relieved of my guilt for failing at our marriage. I knew deep within there was something else for me, I just didn't know what. Sitting in real estate class, and waiting on my divorce to be final I realized there was a greater force at work, and I needed to pay closer attention to what it wanted from me.

"Can I borrow a pen? My name is Jane by the way." The woman behind me had tapped me on the shoulder and brought me back to the present.

"I'm Joy, nice to meet you Jane. Here you go." I said as I handed her a spare pen.

"You want to go walking with me when we have our breaks? It's better than hitting the vending machines" she asked while scribbling on a notebook to make sure the pen worked.

"Sure that sounds great." I turned back around, and a peaceful calm fell over me, I was starting a new career, and I had made a new friend.

Jane and I got to know each other during our class breaks for the next thirty days. Jane was divorced and beginning a new career. We both were confident in our physical appearance, but insecure about our capabilities in making it on our own after being stay-at-home moms for so many years. We spoke often of our same dream, one day loving a man unconditionally, forever. We were very much in the same boat, and I was beginning to think there were probably many more women like us, probably an entire ship.

CHAPTER FIVE
THE ONE THAT GOT AWAY

Real estate school kept me so busy I hadn't bothered to keep up with my Match account. I had no intentions of dating anyone until my divorce was final and somewhat established in my career in real estate. With my divorce hearing scheduled for December twelfth, and my real estate licensing exam on the eighteenth, I had no time for distractions. I went online to turn off my account when a small window popped up to announce an incoming email.

I couldn't believe who I was looking at, "*OMG I know this guy!*" I shouted. His words jumped off the screen and my heart started racing.

"Is this Joy Popma? How are you? I've been looking for you for years. Do you remember me?"

I didn't know him very well except that I worked with him at a bar and grill when I was nineteen. He was a cook while I was a waitress at a baby-boomer *Cheers* style sports bar. He had sandy-blonde hair past his shoulders, even though bartenders and wait staff had to sport the clean-cut Sam Malone look. Landon, was hot and not just because he was in the kitchen, had the body of a Trojan warrior. I tried to sell as much food as I could to my bar patrons so I would have reason to go into the kitchen and flirt with him. Because of him I never called in sick. We went out with co-workers after hours for dollar margaritas. One night, we had a few too many and ended up making out in the parking lot. After that night I had a pretty big crush on him, but he didn't ask me out. I was fired from that job a week after, so I got over the crush much sooner than usual. Most of my crushes became long term boyfriends. Two years later I ran into him at a concert, and I thought we might pick up where we left off.

I was a bit hesitant in responding to his email. I wasn't one to look up old boyfriends, and he really wasn't a boyfriend. However, he was from my past, and had made quite a lasting impression on me. Even while I was married I often thought about him, and wondered what if? *Ugh! I just got through telling myself, I had no place in my life for distractions, and he is a distraction; like a gorgeous spring day at two o'clock on a Friday beckoning me to a patio for a margarita.*

I shot back a message: "Yes of course I remember you, Landon. I noticed your hair is a bit shorter. What happened?"

"Life in the corporate world. I guess we all have to grow up and get an adult job."

"Awe I'm sorry. Hey, do you mind if we talk on the phone? I was about to turn off my Match account." I gave him my number and hit the hide profile tab. Whether he called or not, I was off of Match for a while.

My phone rang. "Hey Joy, It's me Landon. I was thinking maybe we could get together this afternoon and catch up?" He agreed to come to my place for a beer on the patio. It was a perfect fall day, sixty-five degrees, sunshine with a slight breeze. In Texas most of the trees still had their leaves through mid-November. "So what time do you want me?" he asked.

My mind flashed back to how he looked in the past, *now please.* "How about in an hour?"

"Okay, see you then."

I hung up the phone with butterflies in my stomach. I was torn between excitement of having something or someone to look forward to and disappointment in giving into yet another distraction from what my heart wanted, and it wasn't a man right now. I was hoping I could be strong and not get all hot and bothered over him. I remembered being extremely attracted to him and it had been three months since I was tantalizingly teased by Dave, not to mention it had been years since I was intimate with my husband. I was way overdue for some sexual healing. I needed Landon to be a complete turnoff, or I needed the power of God to keep me clear and focused. I was hoping for both; my record for delayed gratification was zero.

I freshened up my mascara and blush, put on some relaxing jeans and a T-shirt. I checked myself in the full-length mirror, *Does this look right for a three o'clock in the afternoon catch up date with a guy I hadn't seen in over twenty years?* The doorbell rang. I took a deep breath as I walked down my little hallway. When I opened the door, I wasn't surprised all that had changed was the length of his golden locks. He still had the body of Adonis.

"Hey how are you? Long time no see." I said as I invited him inside.

"I'm good. I would say you look exactly the same, but you look even better than you did twenty years ago. I wouldn't have thought that was possible."

"You are too kind…or maybe your eyesight is going bad. Whatever the reason, thank you. You don't look so bad either. I see you are still keeping in perfect shape." I said.

"Well thanks, I try." I led the way into the kitchen, which thanks to me busting out some overhanging cabinets when I first moved in, was now an open living concept. I pulled a beer from the fridge and poured myself a glass of red wine. There was a slight lull in the conversation as we both sat down on my white leather sectional sofa.

"Thanks for the beer. And thanks for answering my email. I guess I sent it just in time. You mentioned earlier you were turning off your Match account. Have you found Mr. Right? Or are you getting bombarded with too many men calling on you?"

"No and No. I just realized my decision to join an internet dating site was a bit premature."

He placed his beer on the glass coffee table and looked at me intensely. The silence grew uncomfortable.

"You know Joy, I looked you up many times over the years. I wanted to apologize for not calling you after we ran into each other at that concert. Do you remember?"

"I remember, The Who concert at the Cotton Bowl. It was a great concert… especially because I had run into you. I had to lie to my date because I was gone so long. I told him I had got lost coming back from getting beer, and that I drank both beers while I was lost." I laughed, remembering the lie as one of the worst ones I had ever told, not because it was immoral but because it was lame.

"Yes, it was a great concert, and I couldn't believe I saw you there. I didn't know what had happened to you after you got fired. I wanted to see you after the night in the parking lot; so I came into the bar with some friends to sit in your section, and I was going to ask you out. When you got fired for taking a sip of my margarita, I felt it was my fault. I didn't know if you blamed me for losing your job?"

"Of course I didn't blame you. I was the idiot who sipped on a customer's alcoholic beverage while on the time clock. I was under age too. The only reason I could drink when we all went out after hours was because I had a fake ID. It wasn't the first time I had been fired for breaking the rules." I shook my head remembering how spontaneous and foolish I was.

"Where did you go after you were fired? He asked.

"Well, do you remember Bill the manager? He referred me to a nice upscale restaurant and bar downtown. It was owned by a celebrity and he thought I'd fit in well there. Bill had always liked me and felt bad about having to fire me. Anyway, he was right, I did fit in, and I met my husband at the next job." There was another lull in our conversation.

"So about that night at the concert, we talked about going out, and then I didn't call…I wanted you to know why." He took the last swallow of his beer. "You scared me."

"What? Why?" I asked.

"You were more outgoing and outspoken than I remembered when we worked together. I knew you are a lot of fun and everyone likes you. I liked you and was physically attracted to you, and I never stopped thinking about the night we kissed, which is why it drove me nuts when I couldn't find you for two years. When I went home after the concert, I talked myself out of calling you because we were so different in our personalities. I thought you would eventually walk all over me, and dominate our life together."

"Oh, well, you were probably right. Hey, lucky you, you dodged a bullet, or rather a divorce not getting involved with me. Oh, no I guess you didn't dodge a divorce, but at least not one with me. Oops sorry, there goes my ego again, outspoken and not thinking before saying something rude."

He looked over at me and smiled. "No offense taken, and hey it's the truth. I got involved with a woman a few years later, who was probably just like you. I married her, had two kids, and sometime after the kids, she started treating me like shit, she was never satisfied."

I listened and felt sorry for Landon because it sounded like he was a good guy, like Craig in that he just wanted to love his wife, and be loved back. It seemed so simple when I thought of how love should work like that, and yet it was so hard for me, and obviously for others, to actually manifest unconditional love in a relationship.

"I am starting to think that the two parts of a person, the ego and the higher-self don't really work on the same shift. At least not for me they haven't, and maybe not for your wife while you were married."

"What do you mean?" he asked.

"My ego, the outspoken part of me you mentioned being afraid of, walking all over you, and dominating our lives if we had got together, has been the driving force for me most of my life. I think the ego is meant to be dominate while we are young; for our survival, in competition, and reproduction. It was in a simpler time when the roles of men and women were understood and accepted. In today's world of technological resources, and diverse opportunities for women, even as young girls growing up, we are conflicted and indecisive as to what role we play as an adult. So as a woman, I wanted the life that I dreamed of living, and my dream changed periodically. At first, I wanted to be a famous singer, and when that dream failed, I wanted the perfect life as a wife and a mother. Each dream with my attempt at acquiring it sooner rather than later depended on someone else making it happen for me. But while I depended on someone else, I also wanted to look and feel like I was in control, something special. As the years passed in my marriage and I wasn't looking or feeling special, or having any real control, I started to blame and resent my husband. I knew that he was special, and he was the reason for our livelihood. He was truly in control of his own life because he knew who he was and what he wanted. My ego ran my life like a blue collar worker anticipating winning the lottery, mostly concerned with being safe, stable, and comfortable without putting forth too much effort while wanting fame, fortune, and fun as well. At some point in our lives, our human nature and our higher consciousness are supposed to meet, and have a balance. It took me until a few years ago to become aware of the imbalance between mine." I sat there for a second, really taking in what I had just said to him. It was one of those moments, when I admitted some ugly truth about myself, but instead of feeling guilty I felt renewed, like after going to confession.

"I guess I don't have to worry anymore about what might have been between us, it sounds like you were just like my ex-wife."

I stood up to get another glass of wine, and held my hand out to take his empty bottle. “You know, after I hadn’t heard from you, I wondered why, but then I went on with my life. I met my husband shortly after that, but I had always thought of you as the one that got away.” He stood up and followed me into the kitchen.

“I’m here now, does that count for anything? Speaking of your husband, any plans for getting a divorce?”

“I have filed and my divorce should be final by the end of the year. That is another reason I was getting off of the dating site. The few dates that I went on did not go so well because I was separated. I didn’t like how I was treated or how it made me feel. I decided being separated on a dating site wasn’t conducive for attracting someone to my higher-self. I don’t regret going on those dates, they were how I became aware of the difference between my ego and my higher-self.” I scooched up onto the kitchen counter as he leaned back against the opposite side of my galley kitchen. We just looked at each other for a second and I felt a familiar flutter. I smiled and probably blushed. The moment lasted long enough that I was uncomfortable again with the silence and the look.

“Are you still pursuing your singing career?” He asked.

“Oh no, I stopped pursuing that dream before I got married. I went back to school though, or rather massage school. I became a massage therapist, then I got pregnant and I’ve been a stay-at-home-mom ever since, until now.”

“What do you do now?”

I couldn’t tell if he was genuinely interested or if he was being condescending. *He probably thinks most women bounce from husband to husband with little jobs in between until we snag the next sucker to take care of us. Well, that wasn’t going to be me this time.* I sat up straight and tall and said, “I’ll have my real estate license by the end of the year, so I’m going to be a realtor.”

“Well that’s impressive. I wish you would have been my realtor when I bought my house.” He walked over to the sliding glass door, and peered out over the golf course. “Speaking of houses, do you get this one out of your divorce?”

“I guess you could say that, my soon to be ex cosigned on my loan and supplied the down payment. I moved here after we separated.”

He turned back toward me. “I take it you get along well with your ex?”

"Yes, I do and from what I hear, we are an exception to the rule. We don't hate each other, or wish each other dead. We are actually happy and supportive of each other."

"That sounds like a mature and healthy relationship, what happened in your marriage, if you don't mind me asking?"

I stirred in place on the kitchen counter and said, "It was probably similar to what happened in your marriage, but to really get into it I think we should wait on that conversation. Don't you think so?" He smiled at me and nodded in agreement. "Can we sit outside? The sun is about to set."

"Sure." I jumped off the counter and followed him outside. *Cool, he likes to be outside, and wants to share a sunset together. Score a point for Landon.*

The sun was just starting to set to the west of my back yard. Raspberry, orange, purple, and a golden yellow surrounded us with a fairway of green grass just starting to go dormant. We settled back into two Adirondack chairs sitting side by side.

"What do you like to do for fun these days?" He asked.

"It seems these days I drink wine and read Match profiles. Although, since I've started my real estate career I don't have a lot of time for dating, and after what I've recently experienced, I'm not that interested. I was trying to stay focused, but then you emailed me, now I'm distracted." I winked at him, reached over and squeezed his shoulder.

"I'm a good distraction for you. I promise I won't take up too much of your time. I just accepted a new job, so I'll be pretty busy too. I think we were meant to connect again. We will keep each other focused, and just go out as friends when we have time. Does that sound okay?" He smiled at me and returned the squeeze.

"Just friends, you say? Did I ever tell you my theory on single men and women being just friends? It really isn't possible, there is always one person in the party that is thinking and wanting more." I said shaking my head. I had a feeling seeing him again was either a sign I was to re-connect with him, or a test to see if I was capable of ignoring all sexy, sweet, and fun distractions and get my own life under control. And only then would I be open and ready to fall in love and stay in love. If I could get through the rest of this day and not kiss him, I could manage staying away from him. It wouldn't be like Dave or my first love, Mark. I wasn't obsessed with Landon. I was sexually attracted to him, and fantasized having a little fun with him, but I knew how that gig turned out, and it wasn't in sync with my higher-self, so I needed to keep my ego in check. "So Landon, what do you like to do for fun?"

"I don't play golf, but I do like being outside. I don't drink as much as I use to, but I enjoy an occasional beer or margarita on a nice patio."

"Hey at least we have that in common" I retorted.

"I'm sure we have more than that in common." He looked away from me and stared out at the fairway. His jaw line tightened and his nostrils flared slightly.

"I'm sorry, did I say something wrong?" I asked.

He turned back toward me and said, "Why do I get the impression you are sizing me up for something? Either you are looking for things to be wrong with me so you can dismiss me, and go about your business of not being distracted, or you're trying to guestimate if I'm second husband material."

I tilted my head back and tapped my head against my chair, "Wow! You got all of that from me saying, at least we have that in common? Well, none of what you said was my intention, I was just trying to be funny." We both sat quietly for a moment. I was about to get up and go back inside to end our little uncomfortable date, when he grabbed my hand that was resting on the arm rest. He held it there.

"I'm sorry. You've been honest with me about where you are in your life right now, and with what you are struggling with to achieve on your own. I didn't mean to accuse you of anything. It is probably my own insecurities coming out. This is a really big deal for me, seeing you again." He stood up still holding my hand, and pulled me up to face him. In the last moment of the sunset, he kissed me on the forehead. "Now go study my profile so you will see we have more in common than you think."

I let go of his hand as we started to walk back inside, "I did read your profile, and I know you like sporting events, music concerts, and that you are spiritual, but not religious. We have all of that in common, if that is truly how you live."

"What do you mean by that, if that is how I truly live?"

"What I have discovered in my brief experience on these dating sites is I can't believe everything I read in the profiles. People tend to write what they think others are looking for, and they list attributes they potentially want in their lives, rather than how they presently live their lives."

"Interesting. I thought you were fairly new to this internet dating thing, yet it seems you have a clear perspective on the hypocrisy of it all."

"I don't know about hypocrisy, it might be unawareness of who we truly are and what we really want in a companion. I assume most people, myself included, aren't in tune to our higher-selves most of the time. It's like what I was talking about earlier, we mostly live through our ego."

"I think that was the part of you that scared me before. Maybe the part of me that's attracted to you is attracted to your higher-self, not your ego," he said.

"Maybe. What I believe happens to most of us is we get so busy with work, family, addictions, multimedia, even the convenience of internet dating, and we hardly make time to contemplate what our heart truly desires. We make quick decisions, then suffer the consequences, not really learning from them. We then jump back into another relationship and repeat the same thing all over again. Fifty years might go by, and if we're lucky we figure it out, becoming aware of which part is ego causing the drama and discourse in our lives, and which part is the higher-self wanting love and peace."

"Have you figured it out?

"I'm working on it, I think it is always a work in progress, no one but Jesus accomplished pure divinity. The idea is to find the perfect balance of living more through your heart and less with your head, and that is what I am working on. Which is the other reason I got off Match, I decided to take a break and figure out what is truly important to me; like establishing a career, pursuing my life's purpose, and how I'm to contribute my part in this world. Maybe after I accomplish some part of all of that, I could consider another love relationship, even get married again. Because only then, will I attract the right person to the higher consciousness of me."

"Wow, you've given this a lot of thought. I'd like to be on the sidelines of this journey of self-discovery if you don't mind?" Landon asked.

"I don't mind, but hey, I can't promise you I won't do or say anything that won't piss you off. I am still a very ego-driven being. I'm sure I'll put my foot in my mouth often, and get fiery and defensive sometimes, so watch out."

He pulled me in for a hug at the front door. "Thanks for the warning. What are you doing Friday night, you want to catch a movie?" I tapped him on the back and pulled away from his embrace, "Sure that sounds good. Oh, I have my son with me this weekend."

"That's okay, he can come too, we are just friends, remember?" He headed out to his truck and waved. "I'll call you later," he said over his shoulder. I closed the door and thought, *I've heard that before. Well, if he talks himself out of it again, it's a sign for me to stay away from all men, friends or not.*

♥

CHAPTER SIX
SWIMMING IN THE SINGLE SEA

It was December twelfth and I was heading to the court house to meet my attorney and get my divorce. The day had a clear blue sky with a cold wind that aggressively greeted me when I stepped out of my car. After walking a quarter of a mile from the parking lot to the court house, I wished I'd worn pants instead of the black basic skirt and suit jacket. It wasn't like I needed to look respectable and win. My divorce was simple and amicable.

My attorney and I sat outside the door of the court room. He prepped me on what I would say and do when I stood in front of the judge. Two minutes later we went inside a narrow room with a row of bench seats. We walked to the front where a heavy-set bald man sat shuffling papers from right to left. When we approached his bench, he asked me to state my name and if I were in fact requesting a divorce. I said, "I am." He stamped the formal document requesting the divorce and my attorney and I walked out the side door. That was it. Seventeen years of marriage ended in a matter of minutes. I walked back to my car pushed by the brisk wind. A dull numbness set into my body; I was in shock. The tall buildings of downtown seemed empty and the cars in the street had no sound. I got into my car and burst into tears. The sound of my cry was unfamiliar to me. *Was I doing the right thing? Had I really given it my best to make my marriage work?* Craig was better off without me, and he loved Lonna, it wasn't like I was going to try to get him back. I was truly happy for him, but what was to happen to me? Would I ever truly love a man, in the way I had always imagined?

I want to love a man unconditionally. I want to do things for him without expecting anything in return. I want to hold hands and be affectionate just because, and not just for special occasions. I want to be attracted to him for longer than a couple of years. I want to look forward to going to bed together every night without a television in the bedroom. I want to cook in the kitchen together and pat each other playfully on the butt because we truly were hot for each other. I want to take care of him when he is sick and when he wants to do the same for me. I want to grow old together, rocking in rocking chairs on our front porch, waiting for grandkids to come visit.

I wanted all these things and more, but I hadn't the capacity while being married to Craig. Was it just that we weren't meant to be, or was it me not being capable of loving unconditionally? What was I doing wrong, and why couldn't I make it work with someone as perfect as Craig?

On the way home I stopped at the liquor store and bought three bottles of wine. It was Friday night, I was divorced, single, and alone. Coming out of the liquor store with the buy-six-bottles-and-get-20%-off-value pack I thought, *I'm celebrating, right? I'm going to party like it's 1999. Why am I so depressed? I finally got my divorce and I am free to date whomever I choose. I should call Dave and let him know I'm divorced. Oh, but what if he's already dating someone? I'll unhide my Match profile and change my status to divorced. If he sees it and is still available he'll call.*

I got home, changed into a long lounging dress, opened my $30 bottle of wine and poured myself a fish-bowl size glass. I pulled up my Match account and changed my status. As I sat there I decided I had to change more than my status. I had been changing my life for the better over the past three months, and I wanted to rewrite my profile to reflect those changes. I felt differently now that I was divorced, and I thought, I could handle my new career and a relationship. I was balancing a friendship with Landon and my real estate training hours at my broker's office. It isn't a bad idea getting back on Match, even if Dave doesn't see my divorced status and ask me out again. It could take a while before I meet anyone I'm even interested in.

My new profile:

My divorce was final today December 12th, 2011. I am spending much of my time finding out who I am as a woman. I was married seventeen years. I had been a stay-at-home mom for eleven of those. The identity that I am sure of at this point in my life is that I am a mother. My role as a mother is the greatest purpose I am fulfilling at this time, but I know there is more to discover about myself and my place in this world. I am beginning a career in real estate, so I am on a new and scary journey of long hours and working some weekends. I don't want to be all work, parental responsibilities, and no play. HOWEVER, I am not looking for a shallow and convenient physical connection, so do not respond if this is what you are looking for. What I am ultimately looking for will take time, respect and love, so if you are interested in something like that then email me, and we'll see. ☺

I reviewed what I wrote in my new profile. I knew what I wanted, but how would I get there in my next relationship? I couldn't help but reflect on how my thoughts and behaviors during my relationship with Craig were destructive, keeping my love from ever truly being intimate or unconditional. We were passionate and fun in the beginning but after a couple of years the fire died, and I started to get critical of him and the life we lived together. Even though he provided us with a comfortable lifestyle and was supportive of anything I wanted to do, I was habitually joyless. I would consistently notice all of our differences and keep them in the forefront of my inner dialogue, increasing the distance between us. I quietly resented Craig for not enjoying the outdoors as much as I did, and demeaned him in my mind because he didn't want to spend his weekends updating the house. I often complained we didn't have much in common and that I was bored, yet when he would suggest doing something different like taking cooking classes or going to a play together, I would make excuses why I didn't want to do those things. Instead we'd stay home and drink wine, lots of wine.

Because I didn't efficiently work on my issues, even when I made it known I was trying to, I couldn't truly connect with Craig. Our physical relationship suffered becoming less frequent which then made those few moments when we did connect feel unnatural and awkward. I questioned the authenticity of myself in the relationship daily. I was very negative and resistant about working on myself or the relationship. I felt it was a lost cause. Unfortunately, I often vocalized this to Craig breaking down his own love and trust in the relationship. He would get quiet and would try to give me space, which fueled my ego even more in justifying why we weren't meant to be together. Craig would patiently council me during our bi-yearly communications about our relationship and my unhappiness. He would suggest getting a part time job doing something I enjoyed or going back to school. He even suggested writing a book, something I had always talked about doing after college. Every time he counseled, I grew resentful and angry, disconnecting with him even more. Subconsciously, I knew why I was angry. He was right, I needed to do something for myself. I needed an identity other than being a mother and a wife. I had nothing interesting to bring to the relationship. I blamed him, and used my busyness with the house and raising our son for not pursuing my purpose in life. I was caught in a whirlpool of fear, guilt, and shame, all given life and sustained by my ego.

I struggled with guilt that came from my Catholic upbringing to fight for the marriage, and the guilt of not loving Craig in the way he deserved to be loved. I knew I should set him free to find true love instead of taking care of me. There were arguments in my head that I deserved happiness too, and life was too short not to be happy or in love. I fantasized that being divorced was the answer to all of my problems, and one day I'd be capable of loving someone unconditionally.

Now, here I was divorced, and working toward my own personal happiness with a career. Now all I needed was someone to love. I hit the enter tab for my edited profile to go live. I was hoping Dave would see it instantly and call me. I poured another glass of wine and put on some music that reminded me of the time I spent with Dave out by his pool. I was dancing around my living room to the song *Good Feeling* by Flo Rida. I had a good feeling Dave was going to call, we'd get together, and my life would finally be as it should be. I was building self-worth, gaining self-respect, and love. I no longer needed a man to take care of me, I just wanted a man to love, and that man I wanted was Dave. I had just polished off one bottle of wine when my phone rang. I turned down the music, picked up and saw the name on the screen. It was Landon. *I forgot about Landon.*

"Hey Joy, How'd it go today?"

"Well, I'm divorced...and free to date!" I shouted and twirled around and gestured the letter Z in the air.

"Have you been drinking? He hesitantly asked.

"Yes...Heavily. You want to come join me? I am celebrating!" I started to open a second bottle of wine.

"Sure I can come by for a little while." I continued dancing around and drinking my wine while I waited for Landon to get to my house.

This isn't a good combination to be drunk, dancing to sexy music, and waiting on a hot looking, nice guy that I have kissed before, and I remember the kiss to be pretty good, not to mention it had been a really long time since I last had sex. Plus Dave hadn't even called yet after I changed my status to divorced. It had been three hours already. Screw him. I'll just see where my relationship will go with Landon.

The doorbell rang. I swung open the door, "Hello Baby!" I erupted, and threw my arms around him. I hung onto our embrace as he tried to guide me inside the doorway by backing me up. We stumbled a little and he closed the door behind him with one hand.

"I'm not sure I can handle you tonight," he said as he gently detached my arms from his neck.

"I'm sure you'll do just fine." I said as I grabbed his hand and started to lead him down the hall to my bedroom.

"Where are we going Joy? We are just friends, remember?" I shoved him on to my bed and lay on top of him.

I kissed him but he didn't kiss back. "Kiss me dammit!"

"Joy, you're drunk and I'm not going to do this right now."

"What is wrong with you? We've been dating for the past month or so, I know you are attracted to me, and now that I'm divorced, we can take it to the next level!"

"I didn't think that was the only reason we were remaining just friends?"

"Oh my god! Who cares anymore? Let's see where this could go, and being intimate is part of getting to know each other." I tried to kiss him again, but he pushed me off and got up. He walked down the hallway to the front door. He opened the door and turned toward me and said, "I'll call you tomorrow after you sober up, and you'll be glad we didn't do what you think you want to do right now." Landon walked out to his truck with me following.

"You wouldn't know what to do with me anyway!" I yelled.

"This is the Joy I'm not attracted to, the one I was afraid of all those years ago. Goodbye Joy, I'm done here."

After Landon drove away, I walked back inside and slammed the door. *Whatever, I didn't really want him anyway, my first choice has always been Dave, but that little shit hasn't called either. Oh to hell with them, I'll catch a new man that is better than both of them, and then they'll be sorry.*

I woke up the next morning, remembering bits and pieces of the night before. The damage had been done, I knew that I wouldn't be seeing or speaking to Landon again. I felt really bad. I knew it was my ego that had come out to play, and fight. Alcohol gave my ego an unfair advantage over my higher-self. When I drank too much it was like my ego was on steroids. This was not an original scenario for me, and I was in for a few weeks of guilt and self-deprecation. I thought it best not to call or see Landon unless he reached out to me first.

Landon was smart, and dodged another bullet by not staying with me. I hate this feeling of shame and unworthiness. I want to feel better and leave the past behind me. How do I stop self-sabotaging my relationships? Why do I keep repeating the same mistakes and hurting myself and others? Why can't I just do and say the right things, and live a good life with a good man? I need to begin again, start fresh with people who don't know me or my past. I'll get back on Match and start over.

CHAPTER SEVEN
HOOK, LINE, AND SINKER

To get out of my funk from what had happened with Landon, I turned on my computer to check my Match account. Even though I was disappointed that Dave hadn't responded to my changed status on my profile, I was hopeful that he would soon see it and contact me. I opened my browser and saw that neither of the two emails I had received were from Dave.

Instead they were from two men who stated in their profiles they were ready to settle down and get married again. Both had been divorced for more than two years. I was hesitant. *The ink on my divorce papers isn't even dry yet, and it wouldn't be fair to them if I wasn't ready for marriage again. On the other hand, I deserve a good moral guy and need a second chance at getting my act together. Who knows maybe he might be the ONE. True love shouldn't be restricted to a timeline...right?*

I responded to one of the men who had a daughter attending high school in my son's school district. After we emailed back and forth a couple of times, we scheduled a meet and greet on Thursday night at Mi Cocina. I was excited about my upcoming date. I needed something to take my mind off of the negative and give me hope for the future. I realized now that Landon was the one that got away, but I learned something from it this time. I had no regret of my time spent with him, and someday I would apologize to him for my behavior.

Thursday arrived, and as always I was a little anxious before a first date. On my way to the restaurant I played the pre-date audio through my head; *What if this is the one, and I fall madly in love with him? What if after a year of dating he asks me to marry him and we buy a big house together? If I really love him, I know I could be a great wife and when we go on amazing trips together, it will be romantic like the movies. If he has kids, I will love his kids, he will love my son, the kids will love us and each other, and we will live happily ever after.*

As I pulled into the parking lot, I had to bring myself back into reality. If I went into the date with my fantasies a flutter I was often disappointed when there was little to no connection with my date, leaving me discouraged and depressed.

I walked upstairs to the bar, a very crowded narrow room with a wall of window seats on one side, and the bar spanning the other.

My date must have been watching the door; he jumped out at me and introduced himself. "Hi, I'm Jeff."

I barely said my name and shook his hand, before he turned to a man standing next to him at the bar and said, "This is her, the girl I'm meeting from Match." They high fived each other, and for a moment I was back in high school. Not a great first impression of Jeff. I hoped he was just experiencing first date jitters, but if not, no harm in a sip-and-see.

I sipped on a Mambo Taxi and noticed it wasn't nerves, but high energy that seemed to get the best of Jeff. Thirty minutes into the date, his fidgeting and speaking with his hands, actually his entire body while telling a story had me exhausted and concerned our drinks might spill. I knew I had no right to judge, I've broken many a wine glasses talking with my hands and speaking loudly when I got excited.

I tried to focus on some of his better qualities. He was nice looking in a preppy-school-boy kind of way, wearing a plaid button down shirt, dark denim jeans, and loafers. It was the attire for guys I remembered in the eighties. Unfortunately, I wasn't attracted to it then, and it still wasn't doing anything for me. I made an agreement with myself that I would not judge on physical appearance alone, I wanted to connect on other levels this time around. After hearing his third heroic, marathon-running story, my mind wandered, calculating how quickly I could drink my frozen margarita without getting brain freeze.

I finished my drink, excused myself and went to the ladies room. My inner dialogue was contemplating which excuse I would return to the table with to get me out of this date. When I got back to the table, I apologized for having to cut our date short. I explained to Jeff I had a message from a client that needed me to run some comps for him before the weekend. As Jeff paid the check I thought, *there are some added perks to being a realtor; not having a predictable work schedule, and being somewhat on call for clients provided adequate excuses for getting out of dates early.*

Jeff was a true gentleman and walked me to my car. I held out my hand to shake his and I thanked him for a nice evening. He asked me if I wanted to go out again, and I politely declined saying, I didn't think we were a match, but I appreciated his time and company. I was thankful he didn't ask me why I thought we weren't a match, instead he thanked me for my honesty, and closed my car door behind me. When he walked away my phone rang. I looked down at the screen, and it was Dave. I sat there for a second, my mouth dry and my hands shaking holding my phone.

"Hey Joy, its Dave."

"Hey"

"What are you doing tonight?"

"Um, actually I was on a date."

"Was? It's only eight o'clock, must not have been a good one!" He chuckled. I couldn't decide if Dave was being arrogant, or jealous, but it didn't matter, he had some crazy effect on me. I was tingling all over again at the sound of his voice, the memory of his body next to mine, and his kiss which made me weak in the knees.

"Well, seeing your date ended so early, I was wondering if you might want to come over and hang out with me?"

"I guess I could for a little while. I need to stop and get something to eat first. I haven't eaten dinner yet."

"What? Your date didn't buy you dinner?"

"No. It was a first date. I only do drinks or coffee on a first date. I like to call it a sip-and-see."

"What did you call our first date?" He retorted.

"Amazing," I whispered under my breath. I didn't think he heard me, but from the long silence at the other end of the phone, perhaps he did.

"Hey, I can grill us up a couple of steaks, how does that sound?"

"That sounds great. I'll be there in about twenty minutes, I'm coming from Highland Park Village."

"So does the guy you met tonight live in Highland Park? He must be rich."

"I don't know. I didn't check his bank statements or run his credit. A man's financial worth isn't at the top of my list."

"Really? I thought that was at the top of all women's lists."

"Well, not mine. Hey….I'll see you in a bit." I hung up the phone. It bothered me that he thought all women wanted a man with a lot of money. I was sure there were some women out there looking for a man to take care of them. But I had already lived that life for seventeen years, and although it was comforting not to worry about my financial needs there was always something missing, and I wasn't happy. Maybe Dave had gone through one of those nasty divorces where the wife took him to the cleaners, which was a common story I was hearing from the divorced men I had been meeting lately.

Dave's house in Plano was exactly as I had remembered; clean, elegant, designer décor, and the exotic back yard with the pool and fountains. I walked in and set my purse down on the leather chaise. He closed the front door, came up behind me, turned me around and gave me a sweet gentle kiss. When he pulled back, he looked me in the eyes and said, "I saw that you changed your profile status to divorced, and I had to call." He started sneezing uncontrollably.

"Are you okay?" I asked, and backed further away from him.

"I think it's your perfume. I'm allergic to some kinds. It's usually the expensive ones…my mom and sisters get mad at me when they can't wear their favorite perfumes when I'm around."

"Oh, I'm sorry. Well, what should I do? I guess I could try and wash it off." I motioned toward the bathroom in the direction of the master bedroom, he nodded yes while sneezing, and followed me.

"You know, you will probably have to take a shower. I can give you some sweats to wear. I know that sounds weird, but it really won't help just washing it off, it's all over your clothes." I might ordinarily perceive this as a ploy to get me naked, but his eyes were watering, his nose was stopped up, and he was continually coughing and sneezing. I believed him.

He had left a pair of burgundy sweat pants and a Texas A&M sweatshirt on the bed for me. I put the clothes on and walked out to the kitchen. He had poured a glass of wine and had our dinner on the table. "Wow that looks great on you" he said.

"Thank you, these colors are much more flattering than burnt orange. My sisters went to U.T in Austin, and I refuse to wear those colors. Maroon and white are not bad, I guess I could be an Aggie supporter."

"How's your steak?" he asked.

I nodded yes and gestured with a thumbs up while I finished chewing. I felt so comfortable with Dave, like I had known him forever. Although the sexual passion between us was new, it was easy and natural just being together.

"So what bands do you really like and follow?" he asked.

"Oh, I like so many different types of music, I don't actually follow any one band. When I was a singer, there were a few of my favorite bands whose songs I preferred to sing when my band performed cover tunes, and those bands were Heart, The Police, and U2."

"Seriously, one of your favorite bands is U2? They are like a religion for me. Do you mind if we watch one of their concerts after dinner?"

"Not at all, I would love it. You see after I had my son eleven years ago, I sort of disengaged from following them and buying their music. Once I became a parent, whatever my son wanted to listen to was what was played in the home and car. I tried to influence him with some classic rock which he listened to, but he preferred alternative rock and rap. I think he influenced me more than I did him."

"Well this is your lucky night, I have all the years you missed of U2 in concert." He rummaged through his collection of DVDs like a kid looking for his favorite toy to show off to his friends. He loaded the DVD and I watched as the music and the light show filled the dark media room with a heartbeat and electric energy. I was reminded of a time when I used to listen to record albums for hours with my band. Music had always been a huge part of my life, but it had been more than twenty years since I felt it light up my soul.

When Dave cranked the sound up, the memories of being in a band and performing on stage made me want to sing and dance around. When Dave started to play the air guitar, I took it as my cue to join in and sing and dance along with him. When the concert was over, we both wanted to keep the party going; dancing around the house to all his favorite music mixes. We eventually fell onto the sofa and lay there until four in the morning listening to music, talking about our younger days, people we had relationships with, and how neither of us wanted to get old and boring.

Later that morning, I reluctantly stood at his door not wanting to leave. He pulled me in close and gave me another kiss.

"So it's Friday, what do you have planned for the weekend?" he asked.

"Well, I don't have my son, he is with his Dad. I need to do a little work with my new real estate business, but other than that not much."

"I would like to take you to a nice dinner and maybe back here for some music, dancing, and fun?" He winked at me and patted me on the bottom.

I tried to contain my excitement but failed, I threw my arms around his neck, kissing him multiple times, "Yes! Yes! Yes! Please." I felt I was going to explode butterflies and birds.

We were together that weekend and every weekend for the next six months when we didn't have our kids. We went out to nice dinners or Dave would grill poolside while we listened to music. We watched movies at his house so we could stop and start the movie, allowing time for refreshing cocktails and spontaneous intimacy. During baseball season we watched his favorite team, the St. Louis Cardinals, make it to the World Series against the Texas Rangers. I used to think professional baseball was the most boring sport ever, until he broadened my knowledge of the game and its history.

It had been one year since we had met and we were connecting on multiple levels, some positive and some not so positive. We had similar red flags; we both drank more than we should, had short fuses when we felt threatened, accused, or judged, and had no concept of moderation when having fun. We couldn't get enough of each other in our physical endeavors, finding reasons in the middle of the week to get together and blow off work. I often wondered if we were becoming an addiction, or if we were soul mates with no choice in our extreme attraction to each other.

Our relationship reminded me of the one I had with Mark. Although Mark and my relationship was cut short on account of his ex-girlfriend saying she was pregnant, which she wasn't, we reunited one year later and were inseparable for five years. I had dropped everything to be with him; my high school grades were failing, friendships falling to the way-side, and my relationship with my mom became indignant, which led me to moving out of my house and living with Mark when I was seventeen. We lived, worked, and played together. Our dream was to get signed with a record label and become famous rock stars. We had to work at a fast food pizza place to pay the rent and we lived in a two bedroom apartment with our drummer and his girlfriend for about a year. I put college on hold, and every aspect of my life revolved around his and my dream.

When we broke up, I lost more than my band, roommate, job, and soulmate, I lost my place in my own life. I wallowed in self-pity that following year. I worked in restaurants and bars as a waitress. Deep down in my heart and soul I held onto the dream of being a singer, keeping my voice in shape and writing lyrics, hoping to find another musician-boyfriend to write and record the accompaniment to my lyrics, ensuring my success. I subconsciously fell in love with guys who could help me further my singing career.

For the first time in my life I had fallen in love with a man I did not need anything from, I just wanted to *be* with Dave. However, I wanted to be with Dave so much it was beginning to feel like a need, a need that was a distraction from working to succeed at my career. The more we were together, the more I neglected the other aspects of my life. Even when I wasn't with him, I was thinking about him and what our possible future could be together.

I was falling into old behavioral patterns, putting off what I needed to do for myself, and using love with this man as an excuse for not getting it done. Months went by and I was no closer to becoming financially independent. My greatest weakness, when I felt the onset of failure, was to manipulate the one I was in a relationship with to supplement my inadequacy. This method to my madness historically left me dependent for my survival and happiness on another. I did not want my relationship with Dave to morph into one of necessity, where love was replaced with obligation.

I had close to a year under my belt as a realtor, and I had only one client. I wanted to work hard, proving to Dave I didn't need him to support me, but I was spending too much time having fun with him instead of generating more leads for more clients. We had long lunches at his house; and after our lunches I had to pick up my son from school, so at the end of the day, I realized I hadn't accomplished anything pertaining to my business, and being self-employed, this meant I was unemployed.

Disappointment in myself nagged at me. My inner dialogue beat me up to the point of desperation. *Here you go again, why can't you stay focused on your job? Why can't you say no to Dave and tell him you need to work? Why is it always on his time schedule, and you always have to go to his house? Find your voice, and tell him no sometimes. Are you afraid he won't like you if you aren't always the good time Charlie? Or do what you do best and get him to commit to you and move in together, or better yet get him to marry you, then you won't have to drive over to his house or worry about making your mortgage payment. You can still work, but he could help with the bills, and relieve some of your stress, not cause more for you.*

I was torn, I finally loved a man for him, and not for what he could provide for me. I wanted there to be a way I could have this crazy-sexy-fun love with Dave, and be successful in my career. I knew other people did it, why couldn't I? My mom had recently told me, "When you find the person you don't mind wasting time with, than that is the person you want to grow old with." She had great advice, but unfortunately, I found the one I wanted to waste time with, before I had the time to waste.

I contemplated daily whether this relationship was healthy for me. I had no discipline with time management with Dave in my life, and our late nights of drinking and physical activities had exacerbated a low back injury, turning it into a chronic debilitating one. With only a year into our relationship, I didn't want Dave to think I was weak or needy. I struggled for months with excruciating back pain, getting in and out of cars showing houses to my one client. I dealt with it as best I could during the day, and drank heavily at night numbing my pain to continue having fun with Dave. When I held open houses on the weekends, it was quite challenging being delightful and competent with a hangover. I was physically exhausted, mentally foggy, and emotionally stressed. I found myself while in my car or at home alone wanting to cry, scream, and run away because I had no answers, and felt I had no one to talk to.

I didn't feel my relationship with Dave was strong enough for me to dump all of my complaints and weaknesses on him, he had problems of his own with his ex-wife throwing a wrench in any plans he tried to make with his kids for their summer vacation. I had never been this reserved with any of my relationships, I usually let it be known when I was stressed or unhappy.

One Saturday night Dave and I had been drinking out by the pool for most of the afternoon and I was staying the entire weekend with him. I didn't have any open houses planned for Sunday and my client was out of town, so I wasn't showing any houses. I was free to have a serious conversation with Dave about us cutting back on the frequency of our indulgences for a while until I could stabilize my career and health. We had just come back inside from the pool and settled on the sofa in the media room. I sat up straight and looked over at Dave who was flipping through channels looking for a movie to watch.

"Hey I want to ask you something. You know how we've been dating for about a year now, and I would say we are pretty close, and I know that I love you, and would do anything for you if things got tough. If you had a health issue and I needed to take care of you for a while, I know that I would. What I am trying to ask you is if I were to get sick or something like that where I needed some help, do you think you'd be willing to help me, and take care of me?"

"Are you sick?" he asked while getting up to mix another vodka and soda.

"No, I'm not sick, but I have been struggling with a low back injury that seems to be getting worse from our binge drinking weekends and our late nights of marathon sex. I'm not complaining, I just know I've got to implement some sense of moderation, a healthier balance to our fun. I also need to spend more time working on my real estate career and not coming over in the middle of the week for our long lunches. It's just that when I come over here for our long lunch and then have to pick up Dawson at 3:00 it doesn't leave much time for work."

"Well, to answer the first part of your question, I can't possibly know if I would or could take care of you if you became sick or needed me because that is in the future. I don't know what is at the end of this week, and I really don't care to plan anything beyond it. Your problem Joy, is you overthink everything, instead of being in the moment. Do what you need to do to get your work done, and then we can enjoy our free time doing whatever we want to do. It's that simple."

His answer was logical, and if I was capable of understanding logic at that time, things may have turned out differently. Instead, I was hurt because at that moment I took it that he didn't love me enough to verbally assure me he'd be there for me. I didn't understand. Why could I commit to being there for him if and when he needed me, but he couldn't verbally commit to being there for me?

The fear-based voice in my head was all too familiar, looking for security, trying to create a short cut in fixing all of my problems by manipulating someone else to supply the safety net. In the past, my ego could get the man in my life to supplement what I couldn't or wouldn't do for myself, making me feel safe and happy for a while. What I didn't account for was that Dave had his own issues and insecurities he was dealing with, and his defenses went up immediately, resisting the kind of commitment I was asking for.

The battle of our egos was on. My ego was on a mission to get him to verbally commit to loving me enough that he would take care of me if I needed him to, and to change his lifestyle in helping me discipline mine. His ego fought to uphold his logic of not wanting to plan or commit to anything beyond the present, and to justify his addictions and distractions and continue partying.

When my hangover had worn off later the next day, I called Dave and said I was sorry for how I acted. I was shocked when Dave said during our heated discussion, I had given him a hateful look before I had stormed out of his house. He said that he had only seen that kind of hate in the eyes of his ex-wife, and it truly scared him to think I might be anything like her. I did not know his ex-wife personally, I only knew of what he shared with me, and nothing he had to say about her was good. I was hurt to think he was comparing me to her. I tried to communicate to him that my life at the time was extremely challenging; establishing my career and spending quality time with him, yet I felt my life was spinning out of control.

Dave's response to me was "Joy, I am not what you need. I am a bad influence and I can't be the man that takes care of you. You deserve better than me and you should go find what you need. I'm sorry again."

CHAPTER EIGHT
BEING RELEASED AND FINDING THE CATCH

No matter what my head was telling me, I was hopeful for a reunion with Dave. For now I needed to take responsibility for my own financial needs, health, and personal happiness. My first priority was my chronic back issue and then setting my real estate career on a prosperous path. After a few weeks of visiting the chiropractor and massage therapist, my back was getting better. I was finally adapting to a daily prospecting routine and I had acquired a couple of buyer clients from my new work efforts and improved time management. In two months I had put my career and physical health on a stable path, but I was still missing Dave.

During the first month, I couldn't believe the amount of time I wasted thinking and crying over the thought of losing Dave and wondering, *could I have found a way to manage work, my health and a relationship with him? Did he actually love me, and I was just creating drama where there shouldn't be? Or was I just a physical convenience and fun time for him and he had no long term intentions for us? Was he already dating someone new from Match?*

At the end of the second month, I started filling up my thoughts and free time with extra work, home maintenance, and going out with girlfriends. However, being with my girlfriends often made me miss Dave or made me despise him and want to start dating someone new. Girl power came in numbers and when we would talk about our guy troubles, the ego reached celebrity heights with drama and attitude. I almost always came away empowered, saying to myself, *just forget Dave, don't waste the pretty, and get back out there and load the bases. You're too good for him anyway. He'll never want to get married, he's built a great wall that will never come down. He's a lost cause. It's time to move on and find someone better.*

By the third month after Dave and I broke up, I had made the decision to get back on Match. With much support from my girlfriends, I planned on dating multiple men (loading the bases) to figure out more of who I was, and what I wanted in a companion. I was going to take it slowly, and build on the friendship level before embracing a physical one. This time I would be looking for someone who had a time-consuming profession, didn't drink too much or stay up too late.

It was late fall when I got back on Match and cast a line to a lawyer and a real estate land developer. They both lived in Southlake, far enough from me so the distraction from my work would be minimal. Jaxon, the land developer, was the first one to respond to my email. He was six-foot-four and built like the Terminator. He had beautiful hazel eyes and light brown hair. We had emailed a couple of times before I gave him my number. I wrote in my email that I didn't want to do the standard sip-and-see, I wanted to get out of my comfort zone. He wrote back that he would take care of all the details, and call me in a day or two. I liked his take-charge attitude.

Two days later, the phone rang while I was spreading mulch in my flowerbeds. For a split second, my heart raced as I jumped up to get my phone, thinking or rather hoping, it might be Dave. It was an unknown number. "Hello, this is Joy."

"Hi Joy, Its Jaxon. How are you? Are you ready for our date this Thursday?" He had a slight southern accent, with a clear and slow delivery.

"I'm doing well, and yes I am looking forward to our date. As long as we aren't sky-diving, I think I can handle whatever you've got."

"Well after studying your profile, I figured out how to get you out of your comfort zone, as you requested. We are going country and western dancing."

"Um…Okay…sounds perfect. My new plan for my life right now is to try things I wouldn't ordinarily choose to do. I'm excited, but I'm glad I have a couple of days to prepare. So tell me, what are some of the country music stations on the radio, so I can familiarize myself with the music?"

"You'll be fine, don't you worry about it. Do you own any cowboy boots?"

"Yes…just not sure where they are exactly. So where and what time am I meeting you?"

"We are meeting at Cowboys around 4:30 for sort of a dress rehearsal."

"What?"

"Cowboy's has a beginner progressive three step class on Thursdays. So meet me there around four, we'll have a drink to loosen us up, and then you'll get to learn the most popular dance around. I can't believe you were raised in Texas and have never learned to country dance." He laughed.

"Hey I was a rocker, it wasn't cool for me to even listen to country music when I was younger."

After we confirmed our date plans and hung up the phone, I ran to my bedroom, *what on earth am I going to wear, and where the heck were those cowboy boots?* I found my cowboy boots in the back of my closet and a fringe top I still had from my honeymoon cruise and its country theme night.

I arrived early to Cowboys and when I pulled into the parking lot Jaxon was standing near the entrance waiting for me. I got out of my car and stopped to watch him walk toward me. I could hear my mom's voice in the back of my head, *"Now that's a tall drink of water."* He was wearing a gray cotton blend shirt with the sleeves scrunched up just below his elbows. His jeans were faded and fitted. In the dictionary next to the word man, I imagined a picture of him. He approached me with open arms and I obliged willingly. My cheek brushed the firmness of his chest, and he smelled of a pine tree. So far I was impressed with the way he dressed, smelled, and his warm demeanor.

He escorted me to the dance floor by grabbing my sweaty hand. He looked at me and said, "You're going to be great. Don't worry and just hang on to me." His words were sweet, but ineffective in calming my nerves. While being instructed on the basic steps, he stood behind me with his hand placed at the curve of my back, it was distracting but reassuring. As we started dancing the basic steps together, I was relieved to physically feel he was the dance partner I had never been paired with, a firm lead and tall enough that I could hold on while looking like I knew what I was doing.

Within an hour we learned four of the basic dance progressions and Jaxon maneuvered me like a petit princess around the race-track-style dance floor encircling one of the four service bars. Once we finished the class we danced on our own for a few songs. When my left hip started grabbing my attention over the handsome man holding me in his arms I said, "I think I've got it now. It's not about knowing the dance steps, it's having a partner that can lead. You are the best I've ever had."

"I thought I was your first?" he asked and smiled.

"No. I've done some ballroom dancing before and tried the two step at a wedding reception, but never lucked out in getting a partner such as yourself. I like free-style dancing, you know, night club dancing?"

"Yes. I like to go to the Glass Cactus. Do you ever go there?"

"Sometimes with the girls, but I don't go out dancing too often I'm more of a dance in my kitchen kind of girl."

"I read in your profile, you sang in a rock band? When was that?"

"Oh, it's a long story, but the short of it is I started singing in a cover band when I was fifteen. I later wrote and recorded original music, shopped it with record labels to sign me until I was about twenty-five. I didn't make it, obviously."

"I'm sorry to hear that, I can tell in your voice you were passionate about music and singing. It's too bad you didn't make it, you've got the look with that big curly hair, and those piercing blue eyes. I'm sure you can still rock some black leather pants." He said and winked at me.

"Thank you…I think."

"So how and why did you become a realtor?" He asked.

"I got a divorce, and needed a flexible job, because I was a stay-at-home mom for most of my son's life. I felt the divorce was change enough for him, I didn't want to be working a nine to five job and not be around to help him with homework. I still wanted to be there to pick him up from school every day, and with real estate I can."

"You are a good mom."

"Do you have any kids? It didn't say on your profile, it said ask me later, so I'm asking later!" I laughed.

"No, I don't have any kids, and I've never been married."

"So was that by choice because of a career, or something else?"

"Just hadn't met the right woman." He winked at me and took a sip of his beer. I would have been flattered by his suggestive wink, that I might be the right woman, but considering he was fifty-five I thought it might be a line.

"So how do you like your real estate career so far?" He asked quickly as if to take the focus away from him.

"It's what I needed for flexibility with my schedule, but it's not how I imagined it. It's sort of a stupid story how I chose real estate to be my mid-life career. When I was ten years old, I used to clean the house for my mom, and when I was finished cleaning, I'd get dressed up, and pretend I was a realtor, showing the house to a buyer. You know, taking them through the house and presenting each room, this is the kitchen…and so on." As I outstretched my arm imitating the model women on The Price is Right I knocked over his beer.

"I'm so sorry." I soaked up the little spill with my napkin.

"It's okay. I was about finished anyway."

"So how do you like your job, in land development?" I asked.

"It pays the bills, but I want to do something else, just not sure what yet. I love working out and eating right, so I'm thinking about a career in the health and fitness field."

"You are definitely the picture of a healthy and fit man." I leaned over and squeezed his bicep. Jaxon flexed his muscle in response.

"After I served in the Marines, I had a few engineering jobs, but now I really want to do something I'm passionate about. Working hard at being healthy and looking good is something I enjoy doing every day. Somehow, I want to share that knowledge and joy with others."

"Well then you should, life is too short to not be doing something you love every day. I have recently, well in the past few years, realized how important it is I do something for myself and not depend on someone else to make me happy, which is why I got a divorce." I looked down at my empty high ball and slid it back and forth on the bare table.

"Would you like another drink?" he asked.

"No, I'm good. I still have to work tomorrow."

"I hear ya, so do I."

While he paid the tab, I thought about what Jaxon said, 'wanting to have passion for what he was doing'. *I'm not doing what I am passionate about. Maybe that is the main reason I wasn't happy for very long in my relationships or my careers. I don't just need financial independence, my heart and soul need true passion and purpose in my life.*

We got up to leave the club, and as we walked out to my car he asked, "How about we go do your kind of dancing next, let's say the Glass Cactus next Friday night?"

I looked up into his hazel eyes, grabbed both of his hands and said, "You are on, and then you'll see my true talent." I lifted his arm and did a twirl under it. He pulled me in for another big hug, and then opened my car door.

On my way home, I thought the date with Jaxon went well, but I was determined to line up another with a different guy because this was all about discovering more about myself and what I truly wanted out of my life. I had learned something from my date with Jaxon; I was going to start thinking about what my true passion and purpose was, and start living it.

I hadn't thought of Dave while I was on my date with Jaxon, but as soon as I got into bed I started thinking and worrying, *what was Dave doing, or rather who was he doing? The sooner I fill up my date card the sooner I'll be over him.*

I had a date planned with the attorney for Sunday brunch in Southlake. Of course, I arrived early and waited at the bar. He was late, so I ordered a mimosa. A few seconds later, he poked his fingers in my ribs and spooked me from behind.

"Hi I'm Scott, you must be Joy, or at least I hope you are?"

"Yes I am, nice to meet you Scott." With his rugged boyish look, short spiky brown hair, small beady brown eyes, and five-foot-nine runner-type body frame I immediately thought of the little brother I never had.

We did what all dating advice articles say not to do, we discussed our previous marriages and kids. I found it comforting on first dates with other people who had kids and ex's to talk about them. It breaks the ice, and you learn a lot about a person from what they say about their ex's and kids. Negativity doesn't look good on anyone, so when talking about your ex or your kids, keep it simple and nice.

Scott was a very involved and committed father from what I gathered from our conversation about kids, but his marriage with his ex-wife sounded a lot like mine and Craig's. We talked about his career as an attorney and although he was competent at his job, even aspiring to become partner in the firm he worked for, he often felt he was working so hard because it was what was expected of him. He told me that when he started resenting his wife and kids for keeping him in a daily grind which was stealing the essence of life for him, he knew he had to get out of the marriage for the well-being of his family and for his own sanity. Like me, he thought the marriage had to end before he could make a clean and true change for the better. I connected with Scott because we had similar reasons why our marriages ended, but I wasn't physically attracted to him.

At the end of our date he confessed to me that he had been seeing someone and it was becoming serious, but he liked my profile and pictures and wanted to meet me. I thanked him for his honesty and told him our conversation was entertaining and enlightening and that I thought he was wise to continue on with the relationship he was building with the other woman.

Later that night when I was lying in bed, a profound thought came over me. *Could it be people like Scott, Jaxon and myself, subconsciously keep ourselves distracted from pursuing our true purpose in life by seeking yet another relationship to fill the void?*

Five days after my date with Scott, I was on my second date with Jaxon at the Glass Cactus, dancing to the music of the seventies and eighties. I was seriously trying to have a good time, but in the back of my mind I was wishing I was with Dave. Some days were easier than others; it sucked that I couldn't get over Dave. I excused myself to freshen up after dancing a few songs with Jaxon. While I was in the ladies room, I checked my phone and saw Dave had called and left a message. I couldn't help myself, I called him right back. My heart was pounding and I felt sick, my trembling hand holding the phone while I hit the call symbol.

"Hello?"

"Hey it's me, Joy. Did you call?"

"Yes I did. How are you?" I had no idea what I was doing calling him back. It was an involuntary reaction, like my lungs breathing in air or my heart pumping blood.

"I'm okay. You?" I asked.

"I'm fine, did you get my message? Can I see you again? Tonight maybe?"

"Oh. No."

"No?"

"I meant no I didn't get your message. I just saw that you called, and I called you back." I pulled myself over to a corner of the ladies room to free up the mirror space for all the cleavage-lifting, lipstick-slathering single ladies making themselves irresistible to the coyotes on the other side of the door.

"Well, can I see you tonight?" He asked again. I didn't want to tell him no, but I knew I had to for my own self-respect, not to mention I was on a date.

"I can't see you tonight, I…am on a date right now. I can maybe meet you tomorrow for lunch?"

"Oh, you are always on a date when I call." He said sarcastically.

"Well, what did you expect, I'd be sitting at home pinning over you?"

"No…I was hoping you were." he snickered.

"I really need to get back to my date. Do you want to meet me for lunch?"

"Yes. Can I pick you up at 11:30?"

"Sure, sounds good. I'll see you then." I left the ladies room in a worse state than when I walked in and Jaxon picked up on my mood change right away.

"What happened, did someone use up all your favorite lip gloss?" he asked.

"No, but I do need to tell you something. While I was in the bathroom I received a call from my ex-boyfriend. I think I need to be honest with you and myself. I am still in love with him. I've really tried to get over him and move on, but it has been three months since we broke up and I find myself still thinking about him. I realize now I should not be dating anyone until I'm completely over him. I'm really sorry for wasting your time with me, you deserve someone's full attention."

"Oh, I completely understand Joy. I was engaged about a year ago and it took me six months of being alone and not dating at all before I was over her. It was tough to do, but so worth it, taking the time needed to release the feelings, and those habitual comforts that were with that relationship. If you don't release the relationship in the right way, you will compare everyone you meet and date after, and won't be open to the experience and growth you could have with someone else."

"Wow that makes so much sense. Thank you."

"No problem it was still fun hanging out with you, and I really hope you get over him soon. When you do, don't hesitate to call me" he said as we walked out of the club.

CHAPTER NINE
OFF THE HOOK

Dave picked me up for lunch. The day was overcast and still. We were both quiet in the car ride over to our favorite Greek restaurant. Dave was not accelerating through yellow lights with his fast car this time, and his energy seemed subdued. As we pulled into the parking lot he asked, "Why did you feel the need to start dating so soon after we broke up?"

I was surprised by the disappointment in his eyes and his somber tone. I was caught completely off guard and said the first thing that came to mind, "I can't waste the pretty."

"What does that mean?" he asked, looking at me in a way that made me feel I was being shallow and selfish. After hearing those words out loud I would have to agree with his expression.

"It's just a saying my girlfriends came up with when a relationship isn't going as planned. 'Don't waste the pretty' is supposed to mentally help us move on, get over the discomfort of heartbreak, and get back in the game to find someone who is more compatible with what we are looking for in a mate."

He sat there for a moment looking at me, almost past me, as if he was calculating an algebraic equation. "You women think too much, plan too much, and you get all these ideas of how a relationship should be in your head so you end up missing the actual experiences and the organic evolvement of the relationship. Why can't you just be? Why does everything have to fit the idea of what you think true love is in your head and follow some timeline all you women seem to have for how a relationship progresses to an acceptable level of commitment? It's like someone handed out this manual on relationships when you turned eighteen and told you women not to settle for anything less than that idea."

I could tell Dave was frustrated by the elevated tone in his voice and his hands clenched on the steering wheel. I contemplated for a moment what he said. I was in my head a lot, not only dreaming about how great it would be if we would eventually get married, but when things weren't going my way thoughts about how we wanted different things and he didn't talk about his feelings for me as much as I wanted might mean he wasn't meant for me. These thoughts in my head were monopolizing my time and energy. Time and energy I could have been with him or working. These thoughts in my head had a negative impact on my moods and behaviors, which resulted in our recent break up and in the failures of my past relationships and career endeavors. I was missing the organic evolvement of all aspects of my life by being in my head too much.

"So what are you thinking about now?" he asked.

"Ironically, I was just thinking about what you said about being in my head too much. I've read books about being in the moment, and while reading them I understood the message, but I realize now that I don't live that way. I think what has been most challenging for me with you is I feel the love you have for me when we are together, but when I asked for verbal reassurance from you, you became defensive and indifferent as if being in love with me was a disease you didn't want to catch. I feel we may have some road blocks in our communication sometimes."

"Like what? Give me an example," he asked, sitting up straight and folding his arms across his chest. I could still sense him being defensive but he seemed to want to communicate now and try to understand what went wrong in the past.

"There were times when I wanted to talk to you about our future together not because I was pushing marriage, but because it's fun to dream together when you love someone. It also serves as some reassurance that the person I love and am spending so much of my time with loves me and also wants and envisions a future together. I know that I love you, but it is scary not really knowing if you love me. You don't exactly verbalize it, and when I've initiated any serious talk of love and commitment you back-peddle, avoiding or redirecting the conversation all together."

"Love doesn't always have to be verbalized in order to have it for someone. I think I show you how much I love you by doing things for you like helping you around your house. I think I listen most of the time when you are talking. I think when we are intimate I show you that I love you. Does it feel like I love you when we are together?" He asked.

"Yes it does, most of the time. Sometimes I get the impression you only were with me because I was a fun convenience and wasn't pushing you to get married or live together. It was a blow to my heart when you acted cold and unsympathetic to my concerns and insecurities about my health and well-being. My new life on my own had me feeling vulnerable and weak. In my past relationships no one had cut me off and not given me the verbal reassurance that they cared for me and loved me. You have been quite the unusual mate with your giving when things are fun and carefree, but defensive or restrictive when being asked for deep concern and connection beyond the superficial. I knew then and still do that my problems are my own, but I was hoping you wanted to be morally supportive in my becoming the person I was trying to become. I felt like you didn't want to be bothered with my problems, so it was easier for you to tell me you weren't good enough for me and that I should find someone who would take care of me. Maybe subconsciously I might have been manipulating you into a potential traditional commitment sooner than you or I were ready for, but I never intended on us breaking up because of it." I felt confident in my analysis of our relationship but I anticipated his counter and braced my heart for a jab.

"That's messed up, Joy. I wouldn't think you'd want to manipulate a man into loving you. Look, if we really love each other we will still love each other twenty years from now. You can't go putting conditions on love, like time frames of when a man should propose after one year of dating, or if he truly loves you, he'll tell you every day."

"I get that, and I know in my past I put conditions on my relationships. I am a dreamer, a planner, a romantic, and a bit of a perfectionist, and until now I've always thought that was a good thing. I have fallen in love three times in my life, and for a while I would give of myself completely trying to make his and my life wonderful with what the vision in my head was, but something would happen after a while and I would lose interest, respect, and that loving feeling."

"Joy, I think there are many people who can relate to that, and that is why I just want to take one day at a time, and if you and I are getting along, having fun and treating each other with love and respect than we will probably still be together in twenty years. I am just not in a place right now where I foresee getting married again. If that is what you truly want at the end of the day, then I am not for you, and you really should find someone who does, and don't waste the pretty on me."

"Can I think about it? I'm starving, let's go in and eat." I turned to open the car door and get out. Dave jumped out of the car, ran to my side and closed the door behind me.

Later that evening, I went over to Dave's house and he made us a nice dinner. After making love we lay in bed, spent but rejuvenated. He rolled over to face me, brushing my hair back with his hand. Looking deep into my eyes he said, "I love you."

It was the Thanksgiving holiday when Dave took me to his hometown to meet his parents and sisters. There I learned of his ugly divorce from a marriage that he believed had been strategically preconceived and engineered by his ex-wife. Dave had moved to Dallas after attending Texas A&M. He had a good job and had been working a few years enjoying a successful lifestyle. He returned to his hometown in the Midwest and ran into a woman he knew from high school. The woman, who later became the x-wife, made it her mission to get to know him in a way that would merit a future invite to Dallas. Soon after her visit to Dallas, she moved there. After they dated a couple of years they were married and had two kids. They built a beautiful home and were living the American Dream.

Once they settled into their new home, Dave informed his wife that they would need to cut back on their spending because of the cost of building an extravagant home and having two kids to raise. Shortly after this conversation she served him with divorce papers. When I had met Dave it had been over seven years since his divorce. He held on to the negative memories as if it were yesterday; how he was served the divorce papers at work, and how she fought for more money using their kids as a means to get what she wanted.

The drama between the two of them continued daily, with every decision about the kids down to who was taking them to soccer practice. In the beginning of our relationship, I thought it was a bit immature that he couldn't let go of all the pettiness, allowing her to affect his mood and behavior. When I finally met his kids and I saw how he was with them, I understood it wasn't just about the money, or his pride, it was the constant reminder of the extraction of his parental rights to his kids all the time. He had lost his American Dream. I never realized how unfair a divorce with child custody issues could be to some fathers until I experienced the pain and frustration through Dave's life. I fell in love with him even more as I witnessed his desire and attempts to being an involved and loving father to his kids.

My divorce was easy and cordial, and I had full custody of my son. I couldn't relate to Dave's pain and anger, but I was empathetic. We spoke often of many conflicting situations that involved his kids and his ex-wife. Most of the time I just listened, allowing him to vent. I made a couple of suggestions, like not responding to her spiteful emails, or allowing her to affect his mood and behavior toward his kids when he was with them. Regardless of my suggestions, he cleaved to the negative relationship he had with his ex-wife and the drama that grew from it. Sometimes I sensed resentment toward me for trying to help him release this anger which seemed to restrict his full capacity to love again. He constantly expressed, "This woman will never change: she will always have the upper hand on how my kids are being raised, her mere existence is to make my life miserable."

I didn't want to be one of those women wanting to fix her man, I was trying to accept him as he was and allow our relationship to happen organically. I found it ironic, I needed to let go of my preconceived ideas of our present and future while he needed to let go of his past which affected his present and future relationships with me and his kids. Maybe his anger was his security against ever letting another woman into his life, or having any control over his heart and circumstances. I was worried that his walls would never fully come down, or his heart be fully open to receive all the love I wanted to give him.

I was becoming more involved with Dave and his kids' lives as he was with mine and Dawson's. Dave's daughter was beautiful, smart, talented in music, and athletic in soccer and track. Surprisingly, she looked like she could have been my own daughter, with her long thick wavy brown hair and her big blue eyes. Dave's son was very handsome and quite genius, always working on a new invention in the garage or playing his electric guitar.

I grew fond of his kids and I couldn't stop myself from dreaming of what a perfect little family we could be. I envisioned a wonderful home life with their Dad and me in a healthy, compatible, and loving environment. Then Dave would have that second chance at his American Dream.

What I consistently ignored was that Dave was still reluctant to ever trust another woman in his life in that way. My beautiful dream, or rather expectation of what was best for all of us, was not at all what Dave would allow into his heart or life. I could not make him see and feel what I did.

Through my own experience during my marriage to Craig, I was the person needing my heart opened. I've learned that not everyone is attuned at the same time to unconditional love, and some of us subconsciously sabotage or run from it many times before realizing it is what we're all capable of and destined to live.

Dave and I continued loving and caring for each other according to his be-in-the-moment and go-with-the-flow perspective for another year. He was supportive and informative in helping me learn the prospecting and relationship skills I needed to be a great realtor. He enjoyed talking with my son Dawson about playing football. He ambitiously accomplished honey-do projects around my house. I enjoyed being by his side for hours of watching baseball games, and his partner to kiss every time the Aggies scored a touchdown. I took great interest in all the musical bands he followed. I became close with his extended family and friends, as he did with mine. I wanted to give and do things for him without expecting anything in return. I had never felt this way before for anyone. I finally found what I feared I would never have - loving a man unconditionally, so why couldn't I wrap my head around just being together when we could be together? Why was my ego insisting there be more of a commitment? Why was my thought process continuing to drive a wedge between me and the man I thought I could love unconditionally forever?

I knew better than to bring up anything about changing the status of our relationship. I knew his response would be that I think too much and that there was nothing wrong with what we had going; our occasional long lunch during the work week, and our every now and then blow-out-party-all-night-weekends. I knew in my heart our relationship was more than that, but I couldn't stop my ego from getting in the way of what my heart wanted.

My ego was angling for control and needed a title or a label stating claim on this man so I wouldn't look like a fool or a doormat to family, friends, and society because he was taking longer than usual to commit to me in the traditional way. My ego wanted my own economic pressure of going it alone lifted by his financial help. My heart wanted Dave in my life no matter what to fulfill my desire of loving unconditionally forever.

There was a battle brewing again between my heart and my head, the familiar battle which caused all my confusion and drama in the past. The back and forth of loving then blaming would alter my perspective and my behavior so frequently it sabotaged relationships which could have been opportunities to love unconditionally. I wanted to get off this crazy train my ego kept me on, but when I was drinking alcohol my ego overpowered my heart.

Dave and I had been celebrating most of the afternoon since we had executed a contract on his house which we listed on the market in the early spring. We were five or six vodka sodas into the evening while we were looking online for a high-rise apartment for Dave to rent. I thought this was the perfect opportunity to talk about moving our relationship to the next level.

I casually threw out the idea, "Hey, you know how you're selling your house, so you can move closer to your kids and save money for their cars and college tuitions? Well, I live close to your kids. Why don't you move in with me?"

Dave was sitting in the media room looking for a movie or a game for us to watch. I was sitting at the table in the kitchen with my laptop. He threw down the remote, stood up, and yelled, "Really?" I looked up from my computer and from the look of his face, I knew I had just opened Pandora's Box. "I'm telling you right now that would be the end of us. Combining our lifestyles and kids would destroy us."

"No. I don't think it would. I joined a blended family of nine, so blending a family of five would be a piece of cake." I got up from the table and moved into the media room and stood in front of him.

"Joy, you were five. We have three teenagers, it is completely different! Not to mention you have a three bedroom house, your dog would eat my dog, and I'm allergic to your two cats, remember?"

"We would manage, those things are minor in the grand scale of how much money you could put away, not to mention it would relieve a little financial pressure off of me, splitting the mortgage payment on my house would be less than half the rent for an apartment. Your kids stay with you every other weekend, we could put twin beds in my guest room, and on the weekends when Dawson is at his Dad's house, Kevin could stay in his room." I was trying to stay positive and calm in hopes he would calm down.

"I don't want my kids having to live with us just managing, not having their own room when they come stay with me. Why can't you just be happy with the way things are?" He brushed passed me to make himself another drink.

"I am happy, I just thought it might help us both out financially, and I could help you with taking the kids to their sports and activities, so you could get more work done during the day."

"Joy, you barely have enough time getting your work done for your career and taking your kid where he needs to go, how are you going to fit carpooling mine around? And when would we have our time together? It will literally ruin the unique thing we've got going."

"You are always telling me that you are practical and logical. Consider how much time and gas we would both save not having to drive to each other's houses anymore, and we would have more time together at night and in the morning, you know how much you like our mornings." I winked at him hoping I would lighten the mood.

He slammed his drink down on the glass table next to my laptop and looked at me, "I'm not fucking capable of this right now. If this is what you want, then I'm not for you. You need to go and find someone who wants to get married and take care of you. I'm not good enough for you, you need to find better!"

Dave's words were like a paring knife cutting away all the layers protecting my heart since my first heartbreak. My heart had finally woke up and was open. I felt vulnerable but not weak. I felt confident in how much I loved Dave, but the quiet voice of my heart whispered to me, *it was time for me to leave.* I did not say another word to Dave. I packed up my computer, grabbed my overnight bag and walked out his door.

I didn't call or text Dave the next day, and I knew I wouldn't hear from him either. He was the type that needed forty-eight hours to cool off and reflect on what happened. I preferred to communicate as soon as possible to avoid disrupting the other aspects of my life. I wanted to get back to loving, not worry over lingering uncertainties. My way of communicating wasn't always the right way, in fact I had learned from Dave in prior disagreements that a little time after an argument to discern both sides and the consequences was helpful in avoiding a repeat of the same fight.

Two agonizing weeks went by. It gave me plenty of time to cry, think and pray, until I had an A-HA moment: *It wasn't about me, or what I thought was best in our lives together. Dave wasn't ready, and may never be willing to commit to the kind of relationship I thought we were meant to have, just as I wasn't ready for the life and love I should have had with Craig.* I knew Dave loved me and that his resistance to us moving in together was nothing personal toward me. Dave needed time to release the anger he held onto from his failed marriage, and make peace with the different kind of father/child relationship he has with his kids.

I was beginning to understand that Dave, myself, and probably most people in the world have inherited and acquired hang ups needing to be acknowledged, addressed, and healed before being capable of unconditional love. My long-standing emotional hang ups kept me in a state of concern about myself instead of being present and patient with Dave's past pains. I had made it about myself causing drama and disconnect. I needed to remember: *Life isn't according to me when it involves others, it's according to we.*

CHAPTER ELEVEN
CATCH THE TRUTH AND RELEASE THE ILLUSION

Dave finally answered my call. The closing on his house was just a few days away. Our conversations were brief and cordial about gathering all the documents for the closing. We spent one afternoon together touring his new apartment which was closer to his kids. We hadn't spoken or texted for two weeks after we broke up, yet seeing and speaking with him about business wasn't as difficult as I anticipated.

I was more confident in who I was and how I was living each day. I was living in the present, being patient, and accepting of myself and others. My only choice was to trust God with the higher-good which I recognized because my heart was fully awake and my ego put in its appropriate rank. I was able to see people and situations not as threats or something to control or manipulate, but rather to serve and mediate.

I had acquired two listings and two buyer clients since I had opened myself up to truly help others with no ulterior motives. I was being tested on my newly found presence and patience; two of my client's contracts were becoming heated and complicated thanks to all parties involved being egocentric. I thought the lessons through my relationship with Dave were coming in handy, becoming aware of my own egocentricity helped me acknowledge it in others, making me capable of mediating non-aggressive negotiations.

Closing day. Wrapping up the deal on Dave's house meant I was getting paid, but it also meant I was closing the chapter of our relationship. I wasn't going to try to talk my way back into his life like we had both done in the past. We both needed time for healing and understanding other aspects of our lives, this I knew and accepted, but I wondered what it was that kept drawing us back together. I couldn't help but wonder while sitting next to Dave at the closing table if this would be the last time I saw him, or if we were destined to be together again. *Is there more for me to learn from him? Was there more for him to learn from me?* There were a few times we argued and then discussed it later on when we were relaxed and hadn't been drinking too much. Dave and I were both honest and vulnerable in these conversations and I felt we grew closer. To me it was a sign of real growth in the relationship.

Is there more I could do in helping him get over the hurt and pain of his failed marriage, and the agony he felt not having his kids full time? Am I meant to be with Dave because of his resistance?

His resistance pushed me into becoming independent, competent, and capable of doing more for others.

What if it isn't about finding the ONE and getting married, so family, friends, church, and state would approve of the relationship?

What if it is about being in the moment and not thinking about plans for the future?

What is unconditional love? And am I capable of giving it to Dave or anyone for the rest of my life? Did Dave have it for me?

What conditions did I put on his love for me? And what conditions did he put on my love for him?

Where do I draw the line in the sand if I'm loving unconditionally but I'm not being loved unconditionally?

If Dave and I don't ever get back together, am I supposed to start all over with someone else? Will it be different or end the same? Will I feel the connection with someone else that I feel with Dave? If I don't will I be okay alone?

All these questions raced through my head while Dave signed paperwork at the closing table. I was more preoccupied with the questions in my heart and head instead of paying attention more to the business transaction. Every part of me was afraid I'd never see him again. As he finished, we stood up to shake hands under the title company sign while they snapped a photo of us for my Facebook post.

Walking together out to the parking lot Dave asked if I'd like a celebratory lunch. My heart dropped to my stomach. I drew in a deep breath hoping a heart-wise answer would surface. My heart ached and my head was quiet. I knew nothing was going to change for us as a couple while there were still things we needed to accept and learn as individuals. I needed to be strong and embrace the alone time I had coming.

"I would love to go to lunch and celebrate but I have to meet with my other clients. How about a rain check in about a month, when I come up for air?" I wasn't strong enough to be alone with Dave and hold my ground on spending some time alone. I did have a busy schedule with my other clients but if I didn't get in my car soon I was about to lose it emotionally. I swallowed hard as he looked directly into my eyes.

"Hey, that is great, you're busy. By the way, you did an amazing job with selling my house. Thank you."

"You're welcome." I gave him a hug at my car, trying to hold my emotions together until I could drive away. Tears welled up as I came to the first red light near his house we had just sold. All the memories we made and knowing we weren't going to be making new ones hit me like a levy ready to break.

Three weeks after the closing I sensed I was making some serious progress with overcoming the thoughts and discomfort of Dave out of my life. Any time I started imagining he had already fallen in love with someone and planning to get married and start a new life without me, I immediately stopped those thoughts. Instead, I assured myself it was just my ego drowning out the truth in my heart. *What is meant to happen will happen and I will be happy for Dave if he falls in love and is willing to marry again.* This heart-wise mindset and behavior was hard to stick with at first because my ego liked to get in there and direct occasionally, but as long as I kept from getting drunk, my heart had the last word.

The trick was recognizing the negative thought or feeling and then changing it to the opposite. I had to follow the mindset change with some sort of action like dancing in my living room, or a walk or jog out in nature. I would talk to God, read a spirit enhancing book, or watch an uplifting movie. I listened to *Pastoral Reflections Institute* podcasts, wrote lyrics and sang them around my house. I had all of these enlightening reinforcements to get me through the rough patches making my higher-self stronger and in charge for good.

It didn't hurt that I was swamped with work taking care of other people's worries and concerns on buying or selling their houses, keeping me distracted from my loneliness. My two most challenging real estate transactions were both closing on the same day school let out for summer vacation. I was looking forward to wrapping these deals up and taking Dawson on a trip to Florida.

It was five o'clock on a Friday. With both my transactions closed successfully and getting paid for all my hard work, I was in the mood to celebrate. Dawson was going to his dad's house for a week before our trip to Florida. I changed into my patio perching attire, ripped jean-shorts and a white T-shirt. I cracked open a cold beer and stretched out on the chaise lounge Dave had given me from the pool area at his house.

A soft breeze carried the scent of my confederate vine. It was sweet and sensuous. The flow of golfing foursomes had slowed and it was quiet and private for a change. It was a perfect opportunity to reflect on what I'd accomplished and how I had changed over the past four years.

I bought a house, dabbled in internet dating, got a divorce, earned my real estate license, fell in love, broke up, dabbled in some more dating, back in love again and learned it isn't all about me, made some money as a realtor and helped people in the process release their ego enough to negotiate a win/win deal. I also released my ego and hired my heart to row the boat for the rest of my life.

It seemed like I had accomplished a lot and I should be proud, but it wasn't pride I was feeling; it was enlightenment. All of my mistakes that kept me awake many a nights beating myself up feeling guilty and shameful weren't mistakes, but rather steps in reaching my higher-self and where I am to be at this point in my life.

Looking out at the perfectly manicured grass of the sixth green, I felt a sense of calm and clarity that my life experiences were all part of a quest to understand and manifest unconditional love in my everyday life.

I was feeling like I knew more about myself and felt open and optimistic in attracting someone who would be attracted to the real me. I truly believed my heart was leading the way now. My new awareness equipped me to recognize when my ego tries to distract me from what I truly wanted. I knew now how to change my mindset from egocentric to heart-wise. If my thoughts were negative and not based in the present I stopped the thought process, focusing my attention and actions to the positive and the present. Sitting here in my back yard, my heart was telling me to give the dating thing another try.

After setting up my Match account again, I hit the button to go live. I wasn't going to waste my time scrolling through pages of men, I wanted to see who the universe would dangle in front of me. Exactly a week later, three days before I was leaving on my Florida vacation with my son, I received a most thoughtful email from a man who seemed emotionally and spiritually evolved. I responded without hesitation. I informed him of my upcoming travels and offered my phone number so we could continue communicating while I was gone.

The banter and conversations between us were relevant, fun, and comforting. Even though he was eight years my senior, we had a lot in common and were spiritually compatible. He had read many of the same books on relationships and self-discovery. Our parenting styles were similar since we both had sons. We had a great love for being out in nature and any excuse for having a couple of margaritas on a nice patio.

When I returned home from Florida, I was tan and ready to meet my internet prince charming, Richard. We had planned to meet at a neighborhood bar that was known for its draft beer selection. I arrived early and waited at the front entrance. My phone rang as I made myself comfortable on a window bench facing the door.

"Hi Joy, Richard here, are you already there?"

"Yes. I'm here waiting in the front entrance, where are you?"

"I'm just pulling up to the valet. I'll be right in."

I noticed a sleek black BMW pull up to the valet stand, a tall, broad shouldered man got out of the car and handed the valet his keys. He had the straightest posture I had ever seen and certainly didn't look fifty-five, with a full head of dark brown hair, dark denim jeans, and a light blue button down shirt.

He walked in with a big smile, grabbed my hand and said, "Hey you, I feel like I already know you."

As we made our way into the bar, he held my hand, swinging it back and forth and smiling contently. He ordered our drinks and then tapped his hand on the bar top.

"Let's get right to it. We have covered all the formalities via email and phone calls for the past week, and you texted me that picture of you on the beach. You look awesome by the way, coming out of the ocean."

"Thank you." I said.

"I want to know, what is in that pretty head of yours? I know you've got some kind of movie playing of how you see the rest of your life."

I jolted back and sat up straight. "Wow! That's a doozey of a first question. Actually, for the first time in my life, I don't have a movie playing in my head. I was in a relationship for the past few years and we broke up about three months ago."

"Oh, so you are still licking your wounds then. It takes about six months for every year you were together to truly get over someone."

"Six months for every year? I didn't know that, where is that written?"

"I don't know exactly. I've read so many books on relationship recovery and self-discovery, but it's really from my experience I've learned that it takes some time being alone after a long term relationship breaks up. If you dated this guy three years, you must have been in love, that's going to be a tough one to get over."

"All of my relationships have been long term. Some were tougher to get over than others." I confessed.

"You must not have a problem with commitment. Most of the women I've been dating recently have commitment phobia. They are either angry from a divorce or jaded from being single too long. Both types of women are out there on these internet dating sites looking for the man of their dreams. The problem is, these women are so set in their ways they don't really want a man coming into their lives and changing it. They want the happily ever after but on their terms, and the man is supposed to love and support them but have no say in what he can wear, where they will go on vacation, what friends are allowed to come over to the house, or anything having to do with the house…well you catch my drift. Sorry, I didn't mean to get on my soap box. It's like a man can't win here. I want a serious, committed relationship, but women these days are putting on the brakes, and then if I try and take the go-with-the-flow attitude, they think I can't commit. So what was your issue in your last relationship if you don't mind me asking?"

"Well, I wasn't quite as bad as your description. I have never tried to tell a man how to dress! My issue was the opposite, I made the mistake of asking him to move in with me. At the time I was wanting to find a way to be with him more while I was also trying to establish a career and my financial independence. He needed to put a large sum of money aside for his daughter's college tuition along with wanting to move closer to his kids, so he was selling his house. I assumed after two years of dating exclusively, and I lived near his kids, my idea of moving in together was a win/win."

Richard nodded, "It sounds like a heck of a deal, he should be flattered you wanted to spend more time with him, and thankful you were looking out for his kids' best interest. It doesn't sound like your dreams and ideas were self-involved or out of the ordinary considering how long you had been dating. I think this guy is probably kicking himself right now, or he soon will be when he finds out he lost you to me." He laughed, and held his beer glass up to cheers mine. I looked down at my drink sitting on the bar then I hesitantly raised my glass to his. There was a long silence between us, the first of the evening.

"You are sweet, but in retrospect my ex-boyfriend was right. I think society has us convinced there is an obligation to moving in together or getting married after dating for a certain period of time. Sometimes I felt like family and friends thought I was weak or being treated like a doormat because I wasn't demanding more of a traditional commitment from him. But to be honest with you, I think I had cold feet too." I felt like our conversation was quite serious for a first date but talking out loud about things that hindered Dave and my relationship was making me see Dave's point of view better. Maybe it was wiser to hold off on moving in together and getting married. Richard cleared his throat, snapping my attention back to the present and said, "Maybe you haven't met the right person yet."

"Maybe. So on a different note, what kind of person are you wanting to connect with in your life right now?" I asked.

"That was not a subtle redirection by the way…Well, I've worked really hard to become financially, mentally, emotionally, and spiritually stable. Now all I lack is that special someone to share a fun and exciting life with me." Richard winked at me and fidgeted on his bar stool.

"Did you think you had to get all those aspects of your life stable before you were ready and willing to share a fun and exciting life with someone?"

Richard sat there for a moment before answering. "You know, that's a good question. I'm fifty-five and it was after all the turmoil of my marriage that I really started working on my mental, emotional, and spiritual health. I guess the answer would be yes. I was financially stable before I got married, but the rest of my growth happened during and after my divorce. And now I would say that I'm ready to truly love someone and have her love me, unconditionally!" I was shocked that he used the word unconditionally, and intrigued to hear more of his journey of becoming emotionally and spiritually stable.

"So how evolved does the person you are hoping to connect with need to be or are you willing to work with and through her red flags while living this fun and exciting life? " I asked.

He tapped his hand on the bar and wiggled in his seat. "Wow you have great questions. I've learned through experience not to paint the red flags white, meaning not to ignore the flags and hope they'll just go away because they don't. Like I said earlier, I have been on a few of these dating things and have had a few mini-relationships and let me tell you there are some hot messes out there. I am looking for someone emotionally evolved and spiritual and able to live in the moment gratefully. Oh, and someone who will accept me for how I am and not try and change me or how I dress. Someone like you. You seem to have what I am looking for."

I felt flattered that he thought I was so evolved but I was a bit uncomfortable with the pressure that I may be the one in his mind already. Not to mention I still had plenty of red flags I was working on removing, not painting them white. "Well, I don't know how evolved I am but I do try to live more in the present, and I am more thankful these days for the little things. I don't want to waste any more of my life thinking about what could be, or when I have this, or get married again, I'll finally be happy. That doesn't mean I don't catch myself thinking; I'm not good enough at my job or in shape enough, or if I think my family or friends won't approve of a man that I'm dating because he doesn't make a certain amount of money or doesn't commit to me in a traditional way. I have my weak egocentric moments occasionally. I'm at least aware of them now and I know how to shut off the negative dialogue before it makes me say and do things I'll regret later. I'm consistently happier these days."

"I hear ya. I still struggle with being comfortable in my own shoes and hoping the person I am with will accept and like me for how I am. Would you like another drink?" He pointed to my empty glass.

"No thank you. I've discovered when I've gone on these dates before and I had too much to drink, I wasn't as attentive to the details in the conversation, or aware of any true feelings forming. I want to know if there is an authentic attraction, not an alcohol-induced attraction."

"Yes, I completely agree. I usually only have two beers, and I am almost positive I am attracted to you…authentically." He winked and pushed a water glass in front of me while he took a sip of his second beer.

"So what has been your biggest a-ha since your divorce, the time you've spent alone and dating?" I prodded.

"I probably have at least three a-ha moments for that one. What I have learned, is that men and women perceive most of life's scenarios differently. Where there had been drama and conflict in my relationship there was a lack of open and honest communication. Once I got over the fact her deep issues weren't about me, and mine weren't about her, yet we were responding to each other as if they were, I was capable of working through my insecurities, shame, and guilt. She on the other hand did not, at least not while she was with me."

Listening to Richard I felt guilt and shame all over again remembering how I was when I was married to Craig.

Richard sipped his beer and continued. "For years, both of our thoughts, actions, and reactions to each other were coming from a place of fear, shame, insecurities, and addictions. We existed each day only through our toxic and distracted minds because our hearts were buried beneath all of it. This may sound hopeless and at the end of our relationship I was convinced that it was in ever achieving a mutual, loving relationship.

When one person in the relationship does the internal work and releases the toxic thinking and his heart is no longer distracted, but his partner is not ready or willing to do the same, the relationship becomes unfulfilling and unfair to the one that has changed."

I squirmed in my seat; we had been sitting there a while and my lower back was starting to ache. I thought of Dave and how he was not ready or willing to work through his fear, guilt, shame, addictions, or distractions to love me unconditionally, but I knew in my heart that he loved me and I loved him. I remembered Craig being patient and willing to wait for me for most of the years of our marriage. Could it be that when you truly love someone, even if you are at different places on the path to higher-self living that you patiently and purposely support each other knowing we all will evolve when we are loved and are loving unconditionally?

"So what I gather from what you just told me, it's all about communication. The right kind of communication, open and honest and without ego. If we can talk about the differences in the way we each perceive past, present, and future issues, desires, and vulnerabilities, we are more capable of forgiving, accepting, and growing closer to each other."

Richard's eyes grew wide. "I couldn't have said it better myself. It seems you've already done quite a bit of self-analysis, and that truly is what it takes in becoming more aware of your thoughts and having control over your behavior. The other thing that helps when thinking about your dreams and desires, because we all have them, and it is healthy to have them, is you need to be able to determine if your dreams are coming from your heart or your head. When you have to depend on others to make your dreams come true, or make you happy, then you are dreaming from your head. When you include others who are willing to be involved in your experiences and dreams, and the actual experiences together cause you to feel happy, then that's dreaming and living with your heart."

I stood up to stretch my back and my legs when he gestured to the bartender for the check. "I'm beginning to understand and appreciate that broadening your horizons, gaining knowledge and enjoyment from other people's ideas and dreams can make life much more interesting and fulfilling."

Richard nodded in agreement. "What are you doing tomorrow night?" He asked while signing the tab.

"I think I'm going on an adventure with you!"

"Great, so will you let me pick you up at your house tomorrow for a real date?"

"Yes, I'll text you my address, and you may pick me up like an old-fashioned date."

I went home feeling really good about the kind of man Richard was, and the friendship forming between us, but I was a bit conflicted thinking about how I may not have been loving Dave unconditionally when we were together, and maybe I was jumping the gun again in dating someone new.

CHAPTER TWELVE
UNCOVERING THE DIAMOND WITHIN

Richard was true to what he said, he was looking for someone to share amazing life experiences with. Friday night we went to dinner at an eclectic Mexican restaurant near downtown Dallas. After dinner we went to a historic 1920s beauty shop turned modern day disco playing everything from rap music to classic seventies disco. The energy between us was easy and fun; neither of us were inhibited dancers.

My feet were starting to hurt from the non-stop dancing and I suggested we go. On the way home we stopped off at a nearby park. We sat on one of the park benches surrounding the pond, talking about what a great evening we had.

"I know this is short notice, but I would like to take you to a small music concert tomorrow night. It's this husband and wife band called Johnny Swim. I think you'll love them." Richard took my hand in his and rested it on his thigh.

I turned to face him keeping our hands where he placed them and said, "Yes I'd like that very much, thank you for thinking to take me with you." He leaned in and kissed me softly and followed with another and another. I pulled back to disengage. I didn't want to lead him on with jumping into a physical relationship.

"I think I should be getting home so I can rest for tomorrow night or rather tonight." I pulled my hand out of his and patted him on the leg.

The next night Richard arrived at my house. I felt excited about our date and about having him sit out on my back patio for a pre-date drink. He loved my back yard and settled into one of the patio chairs with a beer. As we got up from the patio table and chairs Richard stopped me suddenly, "Hold it right there! I want to take a picture. You look amazing in that black lace skirt and I want to send it to my youngest son and show him the super-model I'm going out with." He held his phone up to snap a picture as I was turning around. "Just stand with your back toward me and look over your bare shoulder. That shirt is so cool with the shoulders cut out of it. You really should have been a rock star, you've got the look."

"I thought you said a super-model, which is it a rock star or a super-model?" I laughed.

"Okay I got it. This is going in my special picture file."

"Okay…not sure I want to know the purpose for that special file," I said. He casually chuckled and followed me inside.

We pulled up to the valet stand outside a little restaurant that was only as wide as two storefront windows with a single wooden door in the middle. It was a quaint little place, only one room with twelve tables covered in red and white checkered table cloths. Bottles of Chianti lined the shelves along the perimeter of the room, softly lit with an ornate Italian chandelier draped with grapevines. A short, heavy-set, bald man escorted us to a two-top table in the center of the room. Richard glanced at the man and they both nodded, then the man disappeared into the back room.

"I love the ambiance of this place. Are we having Italian tonight?" I asked replacing the napkin the host had respectfully, but too quickly threw on my lap, missing the target.

"No, this place is known for the best steak and lobster in town."

Luigi reappeared with a bottle of red wine, showed the label to Richard and after his approving nod proceeded to open and pour the burgundy liquid into my stemless wine glass.

"You must come here often. They seem to know you and what you want," I said.

"Actually my ex-wife and I used to come here every Sunday. I have only brought one other girl here who I dated for about a year after my divorce, but it didn't work out. That was when I knew I needed more time alone. I wasn't ready to be in a serious relationship."

"And now you are?" I asked. The delicious wine lingered on my pallet sending a warm sensation down the back of my throat. I could feel my cheeks blush.

"Yes, I am very ready to love someone fully and completely and experience an amazing life together. Joy, I am fifty-five and I have reached a point in my life I can do anything. I can start another business if I want, I can travel when and wherever I want. I want to enjoy concerts and world events and do things most people only dream of. Life is too short to live the mundane." He looked at me and refilled my wine glass. The waiter placed a plate of lobster tail, filet, and a baked potato in front of me.

We finished dinner and made it to the concert downtown at The House of Blues just in time for the first song of Johnny Swim. It was standing room only but the venue was small enough for everyone to have a great view of the performance. A young man in his early 30s stood on stage with an electric acoustic guitar over his shoulder. He started the first song strumming vigorously and moving around the stage. The woman with long dark hair swayed back and forth at the back of the stage near the drums. As the band played a few bars the husband and wife duo each made their way over to their mic stands.

They took turns singing verses joining together on the chorus. I was taken back to when I was in my band with Mark. I felt a rush of passion and inspiration. Richard saw I was very in to the music, so he stood behind me and wrapped his arms around me.

We stood there listening to song after song telling of this singing duos' love story. The first few songs described the beginning of their fiery love and passion. Then there were some dark and emotional songs sung with pain and torment of how they struggled because one of them had not been capable of opening his heart completely. One of the songs, called *Over,* described how the woman had reached a point in their relationship when she realized her dream of being together was over after they had broken up multiple times and that she had to stop giving to him what was probably meant for someone new.

I couldn't help but think of Dave and me during that song. Standing there with Richard behind me, I felt the tears coming on. At first, I tried to conceal and wipe the tears away, but then I allowed my feelings to flow. My heart wanted to embrace the moment. It wasn't that I was sad about Dave and I not working out, I was literally crying tears of joy because our relationship was part of my emotional and spiritual growth, and I believed I was part of his and we would one day be together again.

I watched this couple on stage celebrating their love that evolved through it all; the good, the bad, or indifferent. Somehow they fought their way through all the pain and restrictions they had each brought to the relationship. They kept finding their way back to each other until they had chiseled out all the ego to reveal a beautiful diamond of a relationship.

It was fitting the last song of the concert was called *Diamonds,* celebrating that we are all diamonds from dust. I listened as if this was a message from God. I interpreted the lyrics as we all must chip away the illusions concerning materialistic possessions, status, power, religious righteousness, and self-entitlement. If we don't find our way out of this illusory life, we will remain deeply buried, missing our God-enabling transcendence from human nature to Divine. I suddenly realized I couldn't waste the pretty if it came from within. When ego is the driving force, our hearts are covered, but when the heart is awakened and aware of the ego, love can shine through and radiate to everyone. Just as it takes time and patience to mine diamonds, so it takes time mining a heart-driven life in each of us.

The car ride home was quiet. I knew Richard had noticed me getting emotional over a few of the songs, but didn't mention anything about it. I figured we would eventually get around to it in one of our conversations. It was late when we pulled into my driveway. Richard walked me to my front door, gave me a sweet kiss on the cheek and asked, "How about I come over tomorrow and I'll trim those tree limbs that are scraping the top of your roof, and then we can hang out back and talk?"

"Okay. Thank you so much for tonight, I can't tell you how much of an amazing experience it was for me."

"You are very welcome, but I hope you will be able to tell me in detail, maybe tomorrow?"

"Maybe," I smiled and went inside.

It was a beautiful sunny day, a bit hot, but my granddaddy oak tree kept the sitting area cool and shaded. After he finished trimming the tree limbs, I retrieved a couple of beers and as I sat down across from him, he popped the question. "You're not going to break my heart are you?"

I sat up straight and swallowed hard. He had caught me off guard. I felt a rush of blood coloring my face. I had no idea how to answer his question, I liked him, but I thought it was a little soon to be talking about love and heartbreak.

"I can't break your heart." I said.

"How do you figure?" he asked.

"Well, it's like you said on our first date, when you depend on others to make you happy, that is your head, not your heart."

"Good answer, not what I was expecting or wanting to hear, but well played."

"You caught me off guard with that question, and I'm still getting used to this living in the present, not in my head. I'm enjoying our conversations and our dates, but I'm not at that romantic stage yet with us."

"You're right. I think since I met you, I'm guilty of being in my head thinking about all the things and places I want to experience with you. I'm probably moving too fast for you. I keep forgetting you just got out of a long relationship and you probably need some time alone. You may even want time to date a few different people before settling into a serious commitment."

"Well, I don't know about dating multiple people, but you might be right about some time alone. I haven't really done that yet."

"I hate to say it but it was the best thing I did after that one year relationship I was in after my divorce. So hey, how about this? We will continue our relationship as friends because I think mentally and emotionally we are good for each other, and because I want to take you somewhere next Sunday that I think will help you figure out where you are in your life, and what you want."

Richard picked me up Sunday morning a week after we decided we were just going to be friends. I got into his car wearing a long red and black cotton skirt with a black shell top and a matching cardigan.

"Where are we going?" I asked as he jumped in the driver's seat.

"The Potter's House."

"What is that?"

"It's a church, but I call it my spiritual therapy. I think you will get something out of it that will help you begin the next chapter of your life."

We sat up front, taking in the choir before T.D. Jakes came out to speak. His sermon about destiny opened my heart even more. I started thinking about my destiny. How was I going to fulfill my purpose when I didn't know what it was? T.D. Jakes said it was each of our responsibilities to act on our purpose, thrive in it, and share our God-given gift with others. I interpreted the message I had received that day, *if I am not living my true purpose, I will not be truly fulfilled in this lifetime, and I will not be the shining diamond that I was born to be, no matter what or who is a part of my life.*

On the drive back to my house from church Richard asked, "Penny for your thoughts?"

"Oh, I'm just taking it in. Hey, thank you so much for taking me to your place of spiritual therapy. Again, you have given me an amazing experience. I guess what penetrated my heart today was that I am to focus right now on finding and pursuing my God-given purpose."

"So what do you think that is?" Richard asked.

"I'm not sure. As I was listening and thinking in church I remembered moments throughout my life; I've felt an overflowing sensation of joy and happiness when I was involved in doing something creative like singing, dancing, or writing, along with helping others heal physically and emotionally through my massage therapy practice. I recalled in books that I've read about living your purpose, if you were passionate and consistently motivated while doing what you were meant to do, then you were living out your life's purpose. When I think about what I am doing now in my career as a realtor, I don't feel motivated or passionate, so I'm wondering if I am missing my true purpose in life, which scares me. I've actually been wondering for years, what I am meant to contribute in my life time? I don't want to die not fulfilling my part of the big picture."

"Okay, what would you do, if you didn't have to worry about money, and you could pursue a career that's creative and helping others?"

"Well, that is the million dollar question isn't it? I'm sure many people ask themselves that question at least once a year. And if they're not asking that question, they're probably bouncing from job to job, or relationship to relationship trying to fill the void in their life which is likely their purpose not being pursued and carried out."

Richard looked over at me, "I know we are just friends right now, and I am willing to wait as long as it takes for you to find and pursue your purpose, because I know after you do, then our relationship will have a chance to evolve into the love we both want. I will help you in any way I can to do that."

"That is super sweet, and I'm flattered, but I feel deep in my heart I am meant to make this journey alone."

As we pulled into my driveway, Richard looked as if he was searching for the perfect response to my rejection of his offer of waiting for me. I was hesitant to step out of his car, knowing I was leaving behind a potential safety net he might provide me. If I were to silence my heart again and surrender to my ego by taking Richard's offer of the magnificent life he was dangling in front of me, I would continue being distracted from my destiny, eventually repeating my past. I pulled the door handle and stepped out of Richard's car. "Thank you again, and I'll be in touch." I said softly and closed the door.

CHAPTER THIRTEEN
UNCONDITIONAL LOVE

I was into my third sleepless night thinking about my purpose in life. As I reflected on what I had deeply struggled to give in my relationships, I figured my purpose would have something to do with unconditional love. What happened to me between my marriage with Craig and through my relationship with Dave awakened inside of me a vigilant awareness to release everything I had perceived as love in the past, which in my mind was linked with necessity, addiction, and approval.

After my final break up with Dave I experienced profound courage and contentment that settled into my entirety. I no longer felt the need to be admired or in control of others and situations. I was no longer worried or concerned about how I was perceived; if people saw me as weak because of my relationship or financial status, I was not affected. If I had to admit to being wrong for something I did or said, I was willing and happy to apologize, growing from the experience. A humility I had never felt before took over my attitude and perception of myself and others, replacing guilt and worry with forgiveness and trust. Once I was able to change my old thought patterns, I finally understood; my past was not meant for me to repeat but to learn from, and my future was not meant for me to preconceive but to trust in, and my present was meant to serve and love others unconditionally every day.

While I lay there in bed remembering how I had lived most of my life thinking love was contingent upon what my ego's fantastical expectations were, formed from what I thought society, friends, and family expected of and for me, I knew this was not the way to live anymore. There had to be a simple process that would help me and others understand the truth about unconditional love and release the illusion our egos kept us living. *Unconditional love: What is it? How to live it? And how do I share the process of firing the ego and awakening the heart in anyone ready and willing to live their life with unconditional love?* This was my purpose.

I finally got out of bed around 6:00 a.m. Although I was exhausted, I was exhilarated with the idea of getting started on living my true purpose. I poured my morning coffee and sat down to read a daily devotional book Richard had given me, *Jesus Calling*. I had only been reading the daily devotions for a week but already I noticed the clarity and motivation it provided me in staying true to what my heart wanted.

A higher power was guiding me to the people and situations as part of my discovery in living my purpose. It was because of them that I realized the love I had been searching for was not in or from the people I sought relationships with, but rather in and from myself, and what I could give and do for them.

In my marriage I had been on the receiving side of unconditional love, but didn't grasp or implement its true concept of giving it back. I had heard and read about unconditional love through the life and death of Jesus Christ. Jesus dying on the cross was the example of unconditional love I understood as the greatest gift given by God, so that we too are capable and destined to give and receive an endless flow of unconditional love here on earth. However, I didn't understand how to implement this unconditional love into my daily life until after my relationship with Dave had ended.

Thinking about the life of Jesus and his examples of service, bowing down and cleaning the feet of others, healing with the touch of his hands, being present and patient with those not ready to receive the grace and love he was giving, and most importantly, his humbling death, he accomplished his purpose by releasing his humanity and embracing all of his divinity before dying. This was the example to follow. Not that I was going to die on a cross, but I was going to release my ego and stop trying to gain for myself and instead live to serve and help others. Perhaps if I had put the needs and wants of others before mine and been humble in my thoughts and actions in the past, I would have been happy and fulfilled. I realized unconditional love was going beyond the golden rule. Do more for others then you would have them do for you.

Conditions I had previously held in my mind as signs of love like verbalizing I love you regularly, professing a commitment to take care of me, moving in together or getting married because it was expected after a certain period of time together were not examples of unconditional love. Those and many other ways I put conditions on love was my ego trying to control the people and situations in my life. To love Dave or anyone without conditions meant I needed to trust in that love and how I felt in my heart. I needed to turn off what was in my head telling me what I was entitled to, and listen only to my heart which was always telling me to give of myself and not to worry about what I was to receive or how I was perceived by others. My priority was awareness of what triggered my ego, distracting me from loving unconditionally.

My ego fed on my fear of inadequacy, leading me to manipulate others to supplement for my shortcomings. After acknowledging that my inadequacies stemmed from my laziness to learn and implement new ideas and works in my life, I put my heart into action. I structured a plan for facing and overcoming the negative feelings, dialogue, and laziness. It takes time and focus, yet is so worthwhile and a very effective method to instill self-respect and worth.

In the past, my ego did not like responsibility, accountability, or acceptance of how things were, and I always sought out the shortest path to fun, leisure, attention, and acknowledgment. Now, my heart sees responsibility, accountability, and acceptance as a way to be present, acting and reacting according to what is authentically happening, and not what is hypothetically in my head.

My ego was especially stubborn when it came to disciplining myself with drinking, distractions like reality TV, or even internet dating sites. My ego preferred I stay numb, lazy, uninformed, and unaware so when things didn't go my way drama ensued, repeating the cycle all over again. Only by experiencing a traumatic event or a life changing circumstance would I wake up and catch a glimpse of the higher-good my heart wanted to pursue.

Craig and I had tried to have a second child, but I miscarried in the fourth month. After coming home from the hospital, I remember receiving a message from what I sensed was an angel telling me to slow down and be in the moment with my son and family, to know everything gets done in its own time. I listened to this higher power for a while by slowing down and focusing on being in the present. I felt inspired and found my way back toward my true purpose learning and doing things creative and helpful to others. However, when the work I was doing didn't yield success immediately, my ego kicked in with the defeating inner dialogue weakening my focus and I would fail to follow through. Addictions and life-numbing distractions would take over leaving myself and those around me caught in my whirlpool of self-doubt, fear, guilt, and disenchantment.

My ego was uncomfortable with imperfections and vulnerabilities in myself and in others, making me defensive when I was the target and judgmental when others weren't what I expected or behaving how I wanted. My ego was apprehensive about apologizing; I preferred blaming over forgiveness. My ego was so concerned how others perceived me that I portrayed myself as someone I was not simply for the sake of recognition and approval, all while dismissing those who didn't measure up to my ego's expectations. The ego can't stand to be wrong or perceived as weak. In hindsight, I learned the heart embraces imperfections and vulnerabilities because they are opportunities for growth and true intimacy within ourselves and others.

My ego thrived on lack of communication and miscommunication. I can't count how many times I perceived situations incorrectly and didn't have the guts or knowhow to openly communicate my concerns or uncertainties in order to have clarity and growth between myself and others. Lack of communication created drama. Drama induced addictive behaviors kept the egocentric cycle alive. Although, after Dave and I broke up and got back together, there were moments when we shared non-defensive communication, were enlightened by it, and the connection between us grew stronger.

I can't predict that life can be lived without my ego leading the charge, in fact I'm not sure if that is even possible. Ego, to some extent is needed for survival and protection. The ego often drives motivation in athletic, academic, artistic, political competitions, and achievements but is not solely responsible for those endeavors and successes. I believe heart and soul have equal roles as well. The ego stimulates us to look our best and these are all great reasons to hold onto a healthy ego. However, from my own experience of my ego overpowering my heart for many years, I must now be aware of keeping a healthy balance between my heart and my ego. I am much happier with my heart leading the way. When I feel heavy with worry, guilt, shame, fear, and greed, I remember and recite this from *Jesus Calling* by Sarah Young, *"Worries, if indulged, develop into idols. Anxiety gains a life of its own, parasitically infesting your mind."*

In the beginning of being conscious to living with my heart instead of my ego, I had to think of it like I thought of taking care of my lower back injury. I knew the warning signs when my back was about to go out on me, there were quick little jabs of pain that took my breath away alerting me to be aware of what I was doing and how I was doing it. Similarly, the thoughts my ego had, *he hasn't called because he's out flirting with other girls,* or *I won't get that listing because I'm not as experienced as the agents getting the luxury listings,* would cause me moments of doubt, discomfort, and desire to numb myself with alcohol, igniting more drama in my head. The hypothetical worries would then make me feel physically sick or angry, affecting my mood, and if I allowed the thoughts to manifest into communication or action toward others, I would then affect their moods and behaviors, causing discourse, not love or peace.

My awareness of the connection between my thoughts, mood, and actions helped me to consciously stop the negative thought patterns and quickly change it to something positive, *he's busy working so he can take me to a nice dinner this weekend.* This awareness also taught me that the people in my life, such as Dave, had an ego too, that most likely caused the drama and discourse in his life. Once I became aware of the other person's ego and the issues it could cause in their behaviors I was more patient, forgiving, and accepting.

Writing a book like this requires reflection on past mistakes and missed opportunities. I had plenty of them over the past twenty years. Examining the past could have been risky; I could become depressed, discouraged, and given in to many more years of living with my ego-sustaining addictions and materialistic acquisitions. Instead, thank God, I felt more alive and eager to live, once I knew what to be aware of, and how to release the illusion and catch the truth.

Even with all the self-discoveries I've made in the past four years I'm sure I'll still experience struggles, challenges, and heartbreak. Humanity is hard, knowing that we interact with each other mostly through our egos, which is what makes this world challenging with all its pain and suffering. However, when our hearts are awakened and we live more through our higher consciousness, those challenges become life lessons, connecting us all to a higher evolution.

I think part of our lives were meant to be lived through our ego in order to learn forgiveness. I think of forgiveness as flexibility with one's self and with each other. Because of our humanity, we all make egocentric choices causing regression from our divinity. I believe God purposely created us with both an egocentric side which is driven by free-will, and our heart which is ignited with compassion and love. God created forgiveness to connect us. When we forgive our self and others for not being perfect, we accept our humanity, thereby revealing our divinity. When I've caused pain and asked for forgiveness and received it there was a moment of peace and love connecting me to the person I wronged, and vice versa.

Throughout my life I connected to something greater than myself; while looking out at the ocean, writing, dancing, singing, praying, or helping someone in need. I feel it when truly giving of my time and resources to another without expecting anything in return. In times of sadness and loss, sickness and health, work and fun, crying and laughter, I felt oneness with the Divine. I have witnessed in some of the elderly in my life, a demeanor that was light and carefree, not so concerned with their appearance, materialistic possessions, or social status. Their way about them was content, calm, and peaceful.

How and when did these elderly people evolve to such an enlightened state of being? What were the things in their life they gave up or in to? What and who did they forgive or receive forgiveness from? What thought patterns and behaviors did they change? What unselfish acts of service and gratitude did they begin making part of their daily routines? What addictions and distractions did they put an end to? What did they give away to make them lighter and free? How did they let go of all the worry and begin to trust God with the higher-good of their lives?

What I had desired to give in my marriage, and what I finally understood going through my relationship with Dave is in the act of giving unconditional love I'll achieve the state of being content and at peace with myself and the world.

So what is unconditional love? Love without conditions. There are endless examples of how all of us put conditions on our love. I shared some of the conditions I put on love in my story, but there are so many we don't even realize we put on each other every day.

The very first step was to understand the truth about unconditional love so I could recognize the illusion my ego kept presenting in my thoughts, words, and actions. Here are some of the truths which helped me to release my ego and open my heart so I could love unconditionally for the rest of my life:

1) Being present and consciously in the moment, (getting out of my head with all of its hypothetical planning). Expectations are exits from reality, expectations are conditions on love.
2) Attitude: How I feel and act are my choice and responsibility. No one can make me happy, sad, angry, joyful, compassionate, loving, insecure, guilty, hateful, fearful, ashamed, rich, poor, religious, spiritual, kind, trusting, caring, informed, insightful, or enlightened. Only if I allow myself to feel these emotions and decide to act on them could I cause failure, pain, or success and love for myself and others.
3) Acceptance and Forgiveness. (These two truths go hand in hand.) Acceptance of where I am in my life and what I am learning, along with acceptance of others and their position in life. Forgiveness of mishaps and regressions because we are all human.
4) Respect for myself and others. We are all part of the big plan, each and every one of us has a gift meant to contribute in this world, but we aren't all at the same place of enlightenment at the same time.
5) Patience. (This is a biggie!) Everything will get done in its correct time. I had to stop wanting control over people and situations. I had to accept that it wasn't all about me but about the big picture, love and peace.
6) Trust = Strength. My trust in God gives me the strength to do what my heart chooses to do instead of listening to my ego.
7) Communicating with humility and flexibility, and never under the influence of alcohol.
8) All relationships are opportunities to grow and connect. We are both teachers and students in our relationships.
9) Service = Purpose. When I serve others, I live my purpose.

10) Enlightenment = Enchantment. As I continue learning and being present I am enchanted with every day of my life.

Implementing these steps of awareness and heart-wise actions gives me a conscious state of contentment, fulfillment, joy, peace and purpose. I want to pass these steps on to my son and whomever is ready and willing to discipline their ego and open their heart to unconditional love. While writing my story I had no idea I would discover my life's purpose, but now that I have there is no turning back. I am living and promoting the movement of unconditional love worldwide. Living this way is the closest thing to living Heaven on Earth.

I think the grand plan for all of us on this earth is to transcend from humanity into pure divinity. This will take a lifetime and some people believe it takes many lifetimes. The progression can be difficult *and* beautiful at the same time. We are all destined and capable to live our lives with unconditional love for ourselves and others. When we accept that everyone has a part in this amazing life, and respect that we are at different places of growth and awareness, we begin to live a patient, flexible, and peaceful life flowing with unconditional love.

Love is not a game or a dream.
Love is being present and
patient like the flow of a stream.

Joy Popma Gray

♥

EPILOGUE

I stepped out onto my front porch and greeted the cold, early morning November breeze with a deep breath, my face held high to accept the warming sun. Walking up the hill of my street to the fork in the road, I was faced again with the decision; go to the left and walk the route I had been sticking to religiously for the past six months, or go to the right which was my route of preference, not because it was along the high-rise property where Dave now lived, but because I found the Central Park like setting to be therápeutic. I had been avoiding my favorite route because I did not feel emotionally capable of resisting Dave if I ran into him.

Being alone with no distractions I was able to write the first six chapters of my book, discovering in the process, who I am and what my purpose in life is. For the first time in my life I felt me, and I truly loved me.

At the top of the hill my feet went right as it felt authentic. My head was not worried or questioning my intentions, in fact, it was quiet. I was enjoying the hint of fall colors on the trees, the smell of dormant grass, and someone indulging in a morning fire in their fireplace. I had to cross one street which was normally busy with traffic to get to my trail of tranquility, but being 6 a.m. on a Saturday it was deserted and quiet. I did some of my best thinking on my Saturday morning walks; I could breathe clean air and think and talk to myself without anyone noticing the crazy lady walking on the side of the road. (Not that it really mattered anymore what other people thought of me.) I brainstormed most of my daily writing on these walks, and thinking and talking to myself was part of the process.

I wondered about the people who didn't have a therapeutic outlet such as walking or meditating to discern and decipher all their thoughts and issues from their past, present, and dreams for the future. Although my thinking too much is what brought me to divorce, an internet dating site while separated, and had much to do with my breakup with Dave, my recent thoughts had graduated to a positive, progressive level of contemplation. Dave was right about my thinking too much about things I had no control over. He was correct in that living in the present was much better than trying to live the movie in my head. I had worked on eliminating both of those regressive thought patterns and successfully, I replaced them with silence or thoughts of what I can do to help others. I was enjoying the quiet, and all the free time and space to be present listening to and doing things with my son, family, and friends.

I finally got it, or should I say got out of it. I was no longer living in the illusion or matrix. Life isn't about the money, house, vacations, jewelry, furniture, retirement funds, kids, pets, hobbies, addictions, distractions, being right or being famous, admired, acknowledged or even appreciated. It is about being without conditions, just being and authentically accepting, enjoying, and growing from the things and people who come into my life.

I entered the park and lakefront property from the back side toward the wooded trail at the bottom of the lake where it spilled over a small waterfall into a running stream. As I rounded the corner past the last set of cypress trees I saw Dave walking his dog Buddy on the other side of the bridge. At that moment he saw me and waved. We both stepped onto the bridge at the same time and when Buddy saw me he started running toward me, pulling Dave along with him. I started to jog toward them and when I reached Dave I threw my arms around him and said "I've missed you so much." I started to cry and we held our embrace until I gained some composure.

He wiped the tears from my cheeks. "I've missed you too." We walked together, speaking openly about dating other people and realizing we both knew in our hearts that our time together, what we were meant to learn and teach each other, was not finished. We stopped in front of his high-rise apartment building.

"Oh did I mention I'm writing a book?" I asked.

"No. What is it about?" He asked.

"Me…You…Us...And what it is to love unconditionally." I said and leaned against the wall. He looked away from me staring out toward the lake. "Well, actually this book is about how you helped me realize what it is to love someone unconditionally. The next book I write will be about how I actually love someone unconditionally." I said.

Dave turned and faced me. "I'd like to audition for the part of the someone in the next book please!"

I jumped forward and kissed and hugged him with everything I had. "You got the part, you've always had the part!"

www.ingramcontent.com/pod-product-compliance
Lightning Source LLC
Chambersburg PA
CBHW071636050426
42443CB00028B/3347
* 9 7 8 0 9 9 7 8 3 9 1 0 4 *